Writing with Sources

A Guide for Students

Second Edition

Gordon Harvey

Hackett Publishing Company, Inc.
Indianapolis/Cambridge

Copyright © 2008 by Hackett Publishing Company, Inc.

Printed in the United States of America

13 12 11 10 09 08   1 2 3 4 5 6 7 8 9

For further information, please address
   Hackett Publishing Company, Inc.
   P.O. Box 44937
   Indianapolis, Indiana 46244-0937

   www.hackettpublishing.com

Cover design by Abigail Coyle
Composition by William Hartman
Printed at RR Donnelley

Library of Congress Cataloging-in-Publication Data

Harvey, Gordon, 1953–
      Writing with sources : a guide for students /
   Gordon Harvey.—2nd ed.
         p. cm.
      Includes bibliographical references.
      ISBN-13: 978-0-87220-945-9
      ISBN-13: 978-0-87220-944-2 (pbk.)
      1. English language—Rhetoric. 2. Research—Methodology.
   3. Report writing. I. Title.

   PE1478.H37 2008
   808'.042—dc22
                                                    2008010087

Acknowledgments

The present edition continues to benefit from the readers of the first edition and from reading by Edward Baring, Ellen Exner, Bob Hasegawa, Nancy Huang, Maia Macaleavey, Garth McCavana, Sheila Reindl, John Seitz, Suzanne Smith, John Thompson, Cynthia Verba, and Jim Wilkinson.

Contents

Topic Boxes

Preface

Knowledge never stands alone. It builds upon and plays against the knowledge of previous knowers and reporters, whom scholars call *sources*. These are not, in a paper, the source of your argument (you are), but rather of information and ideas that help you discover, support, and articulate that argument.

The questions that most engage you at a university are not the sort that can be answered quickly or resolved to a certainty. You can only suggest the probable truth of your answer by making a strong case that wins the assent of others. Making a strong case to scholarly others—to an audience of students and teachers of a subject who wish to understand it as fully and firmly as possible—involves not only drawing on sources, but taking special care in their use and acknowledgment.

This booklet describes the expectations and techniques for taking care that are common across academic disciplines. It does not discuss how to search for sources, a topic best pursued in the context of particular courses and disciplines. Knowing how sources are used and acknowledged, however, can make it easier to know what you're searching *for*. It can also keep you from taking valuable time away from the creative process of writing. And it can keep you from slipping into plagiarism—an increased danger in era of cut-and-paste technology, when thousands of sources are instantly available through the Internet. But the challenge of writing with sources remains what it always has been. It's the challenge of finding your own voice in the midst of many other voices; of discovering in the constant presence of teachers something that you yourself have to teach; of going beyond the many sources that surround and inform you to become a source yourself.

The principles outlined here apply to Internet and non-Internet sources alike. Even if you believe that you already understand when and how to document sources, you should compare your understanding with what follows. Above all, because some conventions vary between disciplines, don't hesitate to ask your instructor about situations that are unclear to you.

1

The Role of Sources

Almost any record of experience is potentially a source: a text, image, or object; a televised debate or a set of statistics. It becomes a source *of* something, however, only when it plays a particular role in a particular scholar's work. This chapter defines some of the common roles that sources play, in terms of what they provide a scholarly writer and what stance a writer takes toward them. It then considers the importance of using reliable sources and of acknowledging your use of them reliably.

1.1 Sources of What?

A source usually provides a paper with one of two things: (1) it provides *factual data* to interpret and use as evidence, or (2) it provides *ideas about* data, to build upon or dissent from. A distinction is sometimes made on this basis between "primary" and "secondary" sources (see Box A). More specifically, a source of factual data usually provides one of the following:

- *exact text* of a written, spoken, or visual composition (such as that provided in a published edition or on an audio or video recording);
- *statistics or measurements* (such as those tabulated or graphed in a research article);
- a *summary record* of an experience (such as that given in an ethnographic report or eyewitness testimony);
- *information* (such as that assembled in a biography or a textbook).

When a source provides a paper with ideas, it is often providing one of the following:

- a particular *claim* made by another writer about the topic you are addressing, along with the reasoning that supports the claim; or
- a general *concept*—a term, theory, or approach—that has appeared in discussion of other topics and that you apply to your own.

Either facts or ideas, finally, may be brought into a paper in the role of a *comparative case*, which illuminates the main case under consideration by similarity or contrast.

But to make use of a source in any of these ways, a writer must define a stance toward it. The three basic stances you can take toward a source are *yes, no,* and *sort of.* You can affirm or accept it, and say to it, "*Yes, and so. . . .*" You can reject or disagree, and say to it, "*No, rather. . . .*" Or you can qualify or modify the source, and say to it, "*Yes, but . . . ,*" "*Yes, except . . . ,*" or "*Yes, if. . . .*" Your stance toward a source of factual data will often be one of acceptance, although you may call into question the completeness or accuracy of provided facts; your stance toward sources of ideas will vary. All scholars, in making their contribution to the larger understanding of a subject, accept and build on the work of others, but they often discover where their contribution lies through reasoned disagreement with and qualification of that work.

A student writer, Jeff, having done much reading for a term paper on the Civil War, sketched out the following brief proposal to organize his thoughts. Bolded words suggest what a source will be a source *of*; capitalized words suggest the stance that Jeff will take toward it:

> The **claim** of many historians that the North won the war with greater manpower and resources is true, **BUT** such a large event has many contributing causes. Linn and others have **proposed** that Lincoln's leadership was crucial. I will **SUPPORT** this **view BUT** argue that a particularly influential and underestimated aspect of that leadership was his skill at crafting memorable speeches on key occasions to give immediacy to abstract ideals.

Some of the articles that Jeff has read will provide this argument with claims (*proposals, views*) about why the North won. Toward these claims Jeff's stance in his paper will be *"Yes, but."* He won't try, wisely, to refute outright a scholarly consensus about material resources, but rather will qualify the importance claimed for them. Likewise, Jeff will modify the claims made for the importance of Lincoln's leadership by focusing on a specific aspect that he thinks deserves more notice. These moves of qualifying and modifying will provide the motive for his paper. In the rest of his proposal, bolded italics indicate what his sources will be sources of, and capitals indicate the stance Jeff will take toward them:

> I first **ACKNOWLEDGE** the importance of the North's material resources in the outcome of the war, citing statistical ***data***. **BUT** I then give ***examples*** of cases where inspiring leadership influenced military outcomes in the face of resources. Referring especially to the ***example*** of Churchill's galvanizing speeches in WWII, I invoke Simmons's **USEFUL** ***notion*** of "rhetorical turning points." I ***compare*** Lincoln's situation to Churchill's and note the ***fact*** that he **TOO** at key points in a war came up with striking and stirring phrases to unify his audience.
>
> I then analyze the ***details*** of several Lincoln speeches to show how he creates "moral vividness" (in the linguist Denby's **APT TERM**) by finding the right metaphors for the occasion. I trace the effect of his words by analyzing the ***report*** of the speeches in subsequent newspaper accounts. I ***contrast*** these speeches with speeches given by the Southern leader Jefferson Davis that, in a similar situation, do **NOT** have the same effect.
>
> To **REFUTE** a possible objection to my argument, I address the ***claim*** implied in several popular accounts of Lincoln's life that his skill at speaking was not crafted responding to a particular situation but a natural product of his simple and direct personality. I ***compare*** the ***texts*** of early speeches and speeches in draft form to the **QUITE DIFFERENT** speeches Lincoln later gave, to show that he worked deliberately to create his effects. I **DRAW UPON** ***evidence*** of his letters and conversations to show that he was aware of the historic work that his speeches had to do.

Some of the works that Jeff has read will provide his paper with factual data: *report, details, texts, evidence,* and *fact.* They will document the fact that Lincoln did give speeches at key junctures, what exactly Lincoln said and wrote, what concerns were on his mind at the time, and what impact the speeches had. Accepting the accuracy of these sources, Jeff's stance is *"Yes, and so."* He says *"Yes, and so"* also to the applicability of certain general concepts: Simmons's *useful notion* and Denby's *apt term*. And finally, some of Jeff's sources provide comparative cases. He accepts the fundamental comparability of Churchill's situation to Lincoln's, saying *"Yes, and so."* He rejects the comparability of Davis's speeches to Lincoln's (*"No, rather"*) and of Lincoln's drafts with his delivered speeches; and he uses the latter contrast to *refute* the claim that Lincoln's speeches emerged naturally from a homespun character.

It's a sketchy proposal, but writing it forces Jeff to bring his sources into a purposeful order, based on his own thinking, and allows him to move forward. His plan may be too ambitious: he may find he lacks enough information to attribute a precise impact to speeches. Rather than taking on directly the large issue of what won the war, he may end up focusing (as good student papers in the humanities often do) on the workings of one or two primary documents—speeches and letters—in the *context* of the large issue. But because he has sketched a plan in advance, the difficulties will become apparent early—to Jeff himself or to his instructor, class-mates, or others with whom he shares his plan (see section 3.4 #9).

The source roles described are common in college writing of all kinds. Shorter assignments may invite you to work with only one of these source roles. You may be asked to analyze a piece of complex textual data (e.g., argument, poem, novel, film), to agree or disagree with a given claim, to apply a general theory to a particular case, or to compare two works or how two theories apply to a case. Longer assignments, for which you may be required to define your own issue and find your own sources, expect you to use those sources in whatever ways are required to make a persuasive case for your way of looking at the material. Since you will be relatively new to the field in question and can't possibly know all the scholarship, that way of looking isn't expected to be completely new, but it is expected that you'll use sources to say something of your own, not just to repeat them.

[A] "PRIMARY" AND "SECONDARY" SOURCES: Sources called "primary" generally appear in papers as sources of uninterpreted factual data, and those called "secondary" as sources of interpretive ideas; but keep in mind two cautions. First, although a source may be categorized as primary or secondary as it sits on a shelf or in a database, it can often be used as primary in one situation and secondary in another. An article that offers a new interpretation of *Hamlet* would be a secondary source if you were writing a paper on the meaning of that play; if you were writing about a new style in writing literary criticism, the same article would be primary data for you to analyze and use as evidence. Second, the use of the terms *primary* and *secondary* differs across disciplines. Usage in the humanities and fields primarily studying texts follows the basic distinction above. In the empirical sciences, however, *primary sources* are research articles that provide new data but also offer an interpretation of that data. A *secondary source* is an article that summarizes and reviews data from previous research articles, and may or may not offer new interpretations. Because interpretations change rapidly as more data is collected, however, research articles in the sciences do tend to be cited by other papers more often for their results than for their interpretations.

1.2 Citing Reliable Sources

The persuasiveness of a scholarly paper, although it depends on a persuasive deployment of sources in clear roles, also depends on the reliability of the sources being deployed. Suppose Jeff's sources for his paper on Lincoln had turned out to be these:

- for the prevailing view of what won the war: a Confederate War re-enactors Web site and a student report posted on a personal Web site;
- for the facts of Lincoln's life and speaking occasions: Web sites of the Honest Abe Society, a Pennsylvania Battlefield Tours Web site, and a Wikipedia article;
- for early drafts of Lincoln's speeches: a typed handout from Jeff's high school debate class;
- for Davis's speeches: Internet excerpts from an 1880 edition edited by Davis's cousin;
- for his account of Churchill and historical turning points: a summary of Simmons's book in *Time* magazine, a page called "Speaking to Win" on leadership.com, and a year-old Web log.

These sources, neither written nor checked by authorities in the field, out of date in some cases and impossible to consult in other cases, are likely to be inaccurate or at best incomplete in their accounts. And they will be variously influenced by regional bias, by the profit motive, and by a need to be brief and breezy for a popular audience.

A scholarly reader of Jeff's argument would feel let down. Scholarly readers are students or teachers of a subject who seek to understand it and to base their understanding on strong demonstrations. They expect scholarly writers, even writers relatively new to the topic, to be similarly serious seekers. They expect them at least to use the time and the resources at their disposal *as* scholars to make the strongest case they can. This means taking the time to find and use sources that can be trusted to provide full, accurate, and unbiased material and thus provide a stable ground for demonstration. The paper imagined above suggests no serious effort in this regard, but only a quick Google search.

It isn't always easy to know, when you're new to a scholarly field, which sources are serious. But learning to assess the source of one's information, ideas, and attitudes is part of an education in

critical thinking. This assessing habit has become all the more useful now that so much information, and so many ideas and implicit
attitudes, are being assembled, packaged, and repackaged on the
Internet.

You can take your initial cue, in assessing sources, from the kinds
of sources that are assigned as readings in your classes:

- standard, up-to-date editions of texts (the editions used in current articles in the field, whose bibliographies can also be used
  to determine which books and articles are currently important);
- scholarly articles—not from popular magazines but from journals whose contents have been assessed by scholars in the field,
  which therefore reflect ideas that the field takes seriously and
  that handle sources carefully;
- compilations of data—historical, biographical, and statistical—
  that reflect the current state of knowledge in a field.

Sources such as these, which can be trusted to provide accurately
the information and ideas they offer to provide, are readily available
to members of a scholarly community (see Box B). And their notes
and references are better starting points for finding other sources
than a Google search.

It's not the case that anything written for a popular audience,
rather than an academic one, should be distrusted. Because such
works are often both lively *and* reliable, they do appear on college
syllabi. Nor is it always unacceptable, when working on a paper, to
see what a general Web search turns up. Even professors do this—
Google a topic, for example, and visit Wikipedia—as a first pass or
to get very basic or tangential information. In the paper itself, however, they do not depend on the result of casual searches, and neither should you. Doing so increases your risk not only of
plagiarizing (see Chapter 3), but also of making factual errors. The
search brings before you as many unreliable sources as reliable ones
and puts you in the position of having to tell them apart in short
order, which you may not yet know enough about the field to do.
The fact that a Web site gets many hits or has multiple links is no
guarantee that its information is reliable. By the time you discover
that a source is unreliable, you may have already based some of
your thinking on it.

[B] ASSESSING INTERNET SOURCES: The best way to locate reliable sources is to go through a Web site of a scholarly library that gives you access to databases, indices, texts of abstracts and journals, collections of statistics, maps, paintings and photographs, and many other resources, often organized by field. All electronic sources available through these library "portals" are chosen for scholarly authority and reliability. Instructions linked to the library portal page show you how to first find the sources best suited for your search and then how to best search them for the information you want.

Generally, use Web sites and other non-journal and nonbook materials from the Internet only to supplement other sources. When you do use them

- Give priority to those that list their sources (so you can verify the information) or at least list an advisory board of professionals who vet the material.

- If the site doesn't list its sources but still seems serious (i.e., shows no breeziness, carelessness, or bias, and isn't a commercial [*.com*] site), check out the author's professional position and what else he or she has written, and whether the site has a respectable institutional base or is an outgrowth of a long-standing professional organization. You can also directly e-mail the author about the status of a particular piece of information—or post a query.

- Don't use as a source a site that gives no author or supervisory editor.

- When the text on a site is subject to change or erasure, and thus may not be consultable by other readers, try to find a more stable source for the information. If you must use it, either print out the text or have the author send it to you as a personal communication—which you can then cite as such and attach to your paper as an appendix.

If you include non-journal Internet sources in your paper and you have, or think your reader may have, concerns about their reliability or verifiability, include an explanatory note (see section 2.5).

1.3 Citing Sources Reliably

However reliable your sources may be, your reader must be able to see that they're reliable and trust that you are acknowledging them reliably—that you are reliably making clear what comes from you and what comes from your sources. You show this by citing, making a notation in your paper that refers to publication information you provide elsewhere (common methods are described in Chapter 4).

But what constitutes reliability in citing? When should you cite—and why? You should cite on the following occasions:

(a) *Whenever you use factual material—e.g., data, information, testimony, or a report—that you found in a source.* You need to make clear to your readers *who* gathered the information and *where* to find its original form. Even if these matters are common knowledge in the field, if *your* knowledge of them isn't firsthand, your readers need to know where your version of the facts came from.

(b) *Whenever you use ideas—e.g., claims, interpretations, conclusions, or lines of reasoning—arrived at by another person,* so your readers know that you are summarizing thoughts formulated by someone else, whose authority your citation invokes, and whose formulations readers can consult and check against your summary.

(c) *Whenever you use a special concept, term, or theory that you found in a source.*

(d) *Whenever you make use of a source passage's distinctive structure, organizing strategy, or method,* such as the way an argument is divided into distinct parts, sections, or kinds; the way a distinction is made between two aspects of a problem; or with regard to a new procedure for studying some phenomenon (in a text, in the laboratory, or in the field) that was developed by a particular person or group. Citing tells your readers that the strategy or method isn't yours and allows them to consult its original context.

(e) *Whenever you quote verbatim.* When you cite a passage of two or more words in a row, or even a single word (a characterization or label, for example) that is distinctive or striking. Your readers need to be able to verify the accuracy and context of your quotation, and to credit the author of the source for crafting the exact formulation. Words you use verbatim from a source must be put in quotation marks, even if you use only two or three words; it's not enough simply to cite. (If you go on to use the quoted word or phrase repeatedly in your paper, as part of your analytic vocabulary, you don't need to cite it each subsequent time; however, you do need to attribute the terms at the outset.)

You should cite for all of these occasions, even in situations that may seem to you nonstandard. The rules apply, that is, to

- **all uses of sources:** including summaries and paraphrases, even where the source provides only "background" information to your argument (such as historical context or a survey of previous work done);
- **all types of assignments:** including problem sets, computer programs, lab and other reports, collaborative projects, and take-home exams (the fact that your instructor may recognize your use of a course text doesn't change the need to acknowledge it);
- **all types of sources and media:** including numbers, images, graphs and charts, oral communications, films and videos; media including Internet and databases, class sourcebooks and class texts, and lectures.[1]

Finally, although you aren't required to mention the help you have received informally, acknowledging such help is a generous and honest gesture and a good habit to develop (see Box C).

Why cite so scrupulously? The consequences of discovered plagiarism (see section 3.1) are to be avoided, obviously, but doesn't frequent citation weaken a paper by making you seem less thoughtful and too dependent on others? If you find yourself citing sources for almost everything in your paper or even for entire paragraphs, you have a problem. You may be citing "common knowledge" (see Box D) or citing inefficiently (see Box O); or, more likely, you're giving too much rehash of other people's ideas and need to generate more of your own—you need to step beyond your sources. But once

---

1. A lecture is a carefully constructed presentation by an authority in the field, and may itself draw on other authorities; thus, you should cite if you use a distinctive idea, phrase, or piece of information from a lecture. Some instructors may want you to regard their lectures, given for the purposes of their class only, as common knowledge not to be cited. Ask about this before incorporating lecture material.

[C] ACKNOWLEDGING UNCITED SOURCES: Whenever you write a paper of more than a few pages, you draw on many influences: not only sources you can cite as sources of something definite, but also less immediate, less definite sources, such as the lessons of former teachers, conversations or e-mails with friends, class discussions, or an inspiring book you read over the summer. When you have benefited substantially from ideas in sources like these that won't appear in your list of references, you should acknowledge them in a footnote or endnote (see section 2.5). Doing so shows you to be both generous and intellectually self-aware.

Remember, however, that your sources may themselves be using phrases and ideas from their reading or lectures. If you write a paper that depends *heavily* on an idea you heard in conversation with someone, you should check with that person about the source of the idea. Also be aware that no instructor will appreciate your incorporating his or her ideas from conversation verbatim into your paper, but will rather expect you to express the ideas in your own way and to develop them.

you have a case to make, careful citing is at once a service, a moral obligation, and an argumentative advantage.

Your citation says several things to your readers. For one, it says, *"Here is where I found this idea, these words, or this information. Here you can verify the summary of the idea I am giving you or find the full context for the words I have paraphrased or quoted—in case you wish to check them or pursue the matter yourself."* Your citation allows your readers to find in a source what you have found and to make use of it themselves. Such readers are particularly grateful to have it made clear, moreover, exactly what in your paper comes from the source and what comes from you. Your citation also says, *"This person deserves the credit for gathering these materials together or for coming up with these thoughts or words; I hereby acknowledge my indebtedness."* Saying this is only fair to the author in question. Life is short, and he or she has spent many precious hours and days working out the ideas and words that you are casually perusing, assuming that he or she would be fairly credited for them. If you don't credit the author for this work, you implicitly credit yourself for it. If you credit vaguely or sloppily, you create confusion in the minds of others as to what the scholar has accomplished, probably in the process making the accomplishment seem less than it is.

Citing is only fair, also, to the community of students and teachers of which you are a part. It is only fair to other students in your class who fairly acknowledge any help they get from sources. It is only fair to your instructors, who agree to take your ideas seriously—even when they are uninformed and fragmentary—so long as you take the scholarly process seriously by taking yourself seriously as a thinker and as a potential source for other thinkers. When you pretend to have thought or written something that you haven't, you aren't honoring the bargain, and you are in fact treating the process as a game.

Being helpful and fair in your citing also makes your argument stronger. When you analyze data or text from a source, your citation says, *"This scholar has collected the material I'm working with (as you can verify); it's a reliable basis for my conclusions."* When you support or build on a source's idea, it says, *"These learned scholars have found this to be so; it's not just my idiosyncratic opinion or blithe assumption."* When you challenge an idea, it says, *"This learned scholar has this view, as you can verify for yourself: I am not taking on a fool, or creating a straw man."* Citing not only gets you credit for having read these scholars; it also makes your own contribution stand out against the contributions of others—others whose company elevates you.

Reliable citing strengthens your paper, finally, by manifesting intellectual character. It establishes you as not just honest but also helpful, open and generous, serious, careful, and confident enough in your own thinking and reading, and in the intellectual process, to give credit where it is due—to acknowledge other views. Intermittent, casual, sloppy, or vague citing raises suspicion and makes your readers skeptical; ready and consistent citing puts your readers in a generous state of mind, willing to notice and give *you* full credit for the thinking you have done.

[D] "COMMON KNOWLEDGE": Unless you are closely studying a common phrase like "all the world's a stage" or "life, liberty, and the pursuit of happiness," you don't need to cite a source when you use it. These are common locutions, known to all educated readers. Nor do you need to cite information that is either familiar to educated readers or easily available in many general sources (such as encyclopedias, dictionaries, and basic textbooks). The date of Lincoln's Gettysburg Address, the distance to Saturn, the structure of the American Congress, the date of birth of the discoverer of DNA, the fact that Sigmund Freud developed such ideas as the unconscious and the Oedipus complex—such information, in its basic form, is widely accepted and not based on a particular interpretation or point of view; it counts as common knowledge. In the paper excerpted in section 2.2, Jennie doesn't need to cite her passing references to the notion of "oral fixation" (line 6) or the fact that gentlemen used to have an after-dinner cigar separate from the ladies (lines 40–41).

The line between common and uncommon knowledge isn't always clear, but it is your responsibility to take care that an assumption of common knowledge doesn't lead you into plagiarism. If Jennie had gone on to say that the after-dinner cigar ritual occurred even in matriarchal societies—an unfamiliar idea brought to light by the work of certain scholars—she would have needed to cite a source, both to show that the idea has a solid basis and to credit those scholars. If Jennie's argument had mentioned particular aspects of Freud's fixation theory, details that aren't familiar to most readers, she would have needed to cite Freud (or the source for her account of his theory). She would have needed to cite in this paper written for her ethics class, even though the details of Freud's theory *had* been common knowledge in the psychology seminar she took the previous semester. Ideas that are common knowledge in one academic field are often not in other fields. When in doubt on this score, ask—or cite anyway, to be safe.

Note, finally, that when you draw a *great deal* of information from any single source, you should cite that source even if the information is common knowledge, since the source (and its particular way of organizing the information) has made a significant contribution to your paper.

2

Integrating Sources

Whatever role sources play in an argument, they do their work well only if you use them efficiently and always make clear their relationship to your own thinking. This chapter summarizes the basic ways in which sources can appear and basic guidelines for effectively integrating them.

2.1 Ways of Bringing a Source In

At any given point in your paper, a source will appear in one of a few basic forms. You will summarize or paraphrase its main ideas or findings, give its gist, or simply mention it in passing. Or you will reproduce parts of the source exactly, by replication or quotation.

(a) *Summary:* You reduce a source text to its main point and aspects, using your own words but sometimes including quoted words or phrases from the source. When writing an essay about plagiarism in American universities, for example, you might summarize section 1.1 of this book as follows:

> The same source, Harvey notes, can play different roles in different situations, depending on a writer's purposes. He thus suggests that sources are best described by "what they are sources *of*" in a paper (data and ideas of different kinds) and what stance a writer takes toward them (accepting, rejecting, or qualifying).[1]

This style of citation refers your reader to a footnote (see section 4.2) that gives the relevant pages in this book. You will usually be summarizing longer texts than this—whole chapters, articles, or books—so two key requirements, that a summary be both accurate and concise, will present a greater challenge. Two further requirements of summarizing are always to make clear whom or what you are summarizing (*Harvey notes*) and to put your summary in your own words, except for phrases you place in quotation marks (or words in the source that have no real synonyms). This means that, to avoid plagiarizing, you must recast both the language *and* the sentence structure of the source.

(b) *Paraphrase:* With the same requirements in force, your encapsulation follows more closely the source's particular order of presentation or reasoning:

> Sources, Harvey suggests, are best described by the role they play in particular papers. This is a matter both of the kind of material that a source is offering and of what attitude or "stance" a writer takes toward it. While some sources tend to offer mainly factual material, including exact wording, statistics, testimony, and information, others provide ideas, including claims and concepts. Writer stances, he notes, tend to be accepting, rejecting, or qualifying (Harvey 3).

This citation uses in-text, author-page style (see section 4.3). You should encapsulate by paraphrase, rather than summary, when the particular logic or order of a source's presentation is important to your argument. You will sometimes need to paraphrase not to encapsulate a long text, but to clarify a single pithy or difficult statement or concept. Such interpretive or explanatory paraphrasing, especially useful when writing about artistic or philosophical texts, will usually be longer than what it paraphrases. Unpacking the meaning of the short saying used later in this book, to take a trivial example, you might paraphrase thus:

> On this point Harvey invokes the proverb that "a stitch in time saves nine," by which he seems to mean that a step taken early to address a worsening situation will prevent the need for more difficult and elaborate action later on (38).

Your citation refers your reader to the page on which the saying is found, your sentence having made clear with the words *he seems to mean* that the paraphrase is your own.

(c) *Gist:* You give only the main claim or thrust of a work or argument—in a sentence or so—without indicating many or any of its aspects or reasons. To give the gist of section 1.1, you might say that

```
Harvey suggests that sources are best described by
which one of a few basic roles they play in a given
paper (2008).
```

This citation and those in the following examples illustrate in-text author-year style (see section 4.4).

(d) *Mention:* You refer to the source in passing, invoking it as part of a general characterization:

```
Some analysts, such as Harvey, stress the roles that
different sources play (2008).
```

(e) *Citation Only:* You relegate the name of the source to a parenthetical citation or footnote:

```
Still other analysts see the roles that sources play
as the determining factor (Harvey, 2008).
```

(f) *Exact reproduction:* You replicate exactly an element of another source, such as a data table or a figure (e.g., a chart, graph, diagram, or map), or you quote exactly the words of the source, either embedding those words in one of your sentences or (if more than four lines of type) quoting them as an indented block. Reasons to quote a source directly include the following:

- The source author has made a point so clearly and concisely that it can't be expressed any better.
- A certain phrase or sentence in the source is particularly vivid or striking, or especially typical or representative of some phenomenon you are discussing.
- An important passage is sufficiently difficult, dense, or rich that it requires you to analyze it closely, which in turn requires that the passage be produced so the reader can follow your analysis.
- A claim you are making is such that the doubting reader will want to hear exactly what the source said. This will often be the case when you criticize or disagree with a source; your reader wants to feel sure you aren't misrepresenting the source—or creating a straw man (or woman). In addition, you need to quote *enough* of the source so that the context and meaning are clear.

[E] MENTIONING A TITLE IN A PAPER: Italicize the title of a book (as in line 10 of Jennie's paper) or collection, journal or newspaper, play, long poem, film, musical composition, or artwork. Put in quotation marks the title of an individual article, chapter, essay, story, or poem. Don't italicize the Bible or its books, or legal documents like the Constitution. For an italicized title that contains another title, indicate the latter by underlining (*The Making of* <u>*The Origin of Species*</u>) or by un-italicizing (*The Making of* The Origin of Species).

2.2 Three Basic Principles

Depending on the academic field, sources appear in some of these forms more frequently than in others. Direct quotation, for example, is all but essential in literary papers, but is rare in the sciences and data-based social sciences. Three basic principles, however, should govern your thinking about how sources appear in any paper.

FIRST PRINCIPLE: *Use sources as concisely as possible, so your own thinking isn't crowded out by your presentation of other people's thinking and your own voice lost in your quoting of other voices.* This means that you should mention or summarize your source, perhaps quoting a vivid phrase or two, unless you have a good reason to paraphrase closely or quote more extensively.

SECOND PRINCIPLE: *Never leave your reader in doubt as to when you are speaking and when you are relying on material from a source.* Avoid ambiguity by (a) citing the source immediately after drawing on it, but also (if discussing the source or quoting it directly) by (b) announcing the source in your own sentence or phrases preceding its appearance and, for extensive quotation, by (c) following up its appearance with commentary about it or development from it that makes clear where your contribution starts, referring back to the source by name (*Compton's comment is questionable in several ways . . .*). Although you need not restate the name of your source where it's obvious, if your summary of it continues for many sentences you should remind your reader that you are still summarizing, not interpreting or developing.

You need not give the name or names of a source in advance when you merely mention it but don't quote it or discuss it at length (see the use of Bell, Schmidt, and Wills in the following excerpt). Be careful, however, that your citation doesn't come so late in your paragraph that it creates ambiguity about which ideas are yours and which are the source's.

THIRD PRINCIPLE: *Always make clear how each source you introduce into your paper relates to your argument.* This means indicating to your reader, in the words leading up to your summary, paraphrase, or quotation of a source, or in the sentences that follow and reflect on it (or both), what you want your reader to notice or focus on in the source and what your stance toward it is (see section 1.1). See also section 2.3d.

Notice how a student writer, Jennie, observes these three principles in this excerpt from a paper about why people engage in self-destructive behaviors like smoking and drinking:

```
1    Scientists distinguish between "proximate" and
2    "ultimate" explanations (Bell 600). An ultimate, long-
3    range explanation of smoking, based on a study of
4    human evolution, has greater appeal for many people
5    than a more localized, proximate explanation — like
6    chemical changes in the body or an oral fixation. But
7    ultimate explanations may conflict with proximate
8    evidence that seems more obvious, as does the
9    explanation proposed by physiologist Jared Diamond in
10   his recent book The Third Chimpanzee. Diamond cites
11   the theory of zoologist Amotz Zahavi that self-
12   endangering behaviors in animals (such as a male bird
13   displaying a big tail and a loud song to a female) may be
14   at once a signal and a proof of superior powers (196).
15   Such a bird has proved, writes Diamond, "that he must
16   be especially good at escaping predators, finding food,
17   resisting disease; the bigger the handicap, the more
18   rigorous the test he has passed." Humans share the
19   same instinct that makes birds give dangerous displays,
20   he suggests; and risky human actions, including the use
21   of drugs, are designed to impress potential mates and
22   competitors in the way Zahavi suggests risky animal
23   actions are (198). Diamond's characterization of the
24   message that teenagers send by smoking and drinking
25   creates an image of a strutting animal:

26       I'm strong and I'm superior. Even to take drugs
27       once or twice, I must be strong enough to get past
```

28   the burning, choking sensation of my first puff on
29   a cigarette, or to get past the misery of my first
30   hangover. To do it chronically and remain alive
31   and healthy, I must be superior. (199)

32 An apparent problem with this ultimate, evolutionary
33 explanation of smoking, however, is that people were
34 smoking long before they knew it was dangerous, before
35 they knew that doing it chronically made it harder to
36 "remain alive and healthy." Public concern about
37 smoking did not appear until the 1950s (Schmidt 29).
38 Before that, moreover, many people smoked in private —
39 removed from potential mates they might impress; men
40 had a quiet pipe by the fire or actually left the ladies (or
41 the ladies left them) to have a cigar after dinner. Finally,
42 Native American peoples smoked tobacco for centuries,
43 apparently for its pleasantly elevating effect (Wills 77).

In terms of the source roles mentioned in section 1.1, this excerpt
breaks down as follows: Bell provides Jennie with a general concept
(a distinction between types of explanation), which she accepts and
applies to her own topic; Diamond provides her with a claim and an
argument, which she rejects; and Schmidt and Wills provide her
with information that she accepts as factual and as providing support for her claims that concern about smoking is recent and that
Native Americans smoked tobacco for its pleasant effect. Later in
the paper she uses, as sources of primary text, interviews she conducted with adolescents about their first smoking and drinking
experiences.

     In each case, Jennie uses her sources concisely and clearly. She
summarizes, in passing, Bell's conceptual distinction. She reduces
Diamond's 10-page argument about smoking and drinking to a few
sentences and short quotations, and she merely refers her readers to
Schmidt and Wills. She makes clear the relevance of the summary of
Diamond to her argument in the sentence at lines 6–8 that leads up
to the summary, providing an argumentative context for it (*But ultimate explanations may conflict with proximate evidence*) and then again
by explicitly discussing the summarized material in the sentences
following the quotation (*An apparent problem with this ultimate, evolutionary explanation*). Because her summary of Diamond continues for
several lines, she reminds the reader at the beginning of line 20 (*he
suggests*) that she is still summarizing. She also has been careful to
paraphrase at those times in her summary when she may have been
tempted merely to repeat her source's words. She paraphrases this
sentence in Diamond's book:

```
It seems to me that Zahavi's theory applies to many
costly or dangerous human behaviors aimed at
achieving status in general or at sexual benefits in
particular.
```

Her paraphrase, at lines 20–23, is different in both language and sentence structure:

```
risky human actions, including the use of drugs, are
designed to impress potential mates and competitors
in the way Zahavi suggests risky animal actions are
(198).
```

Jennie's paragraph also illustrates one further rule: *mention the nature or professional status of your source if it's distinctive*. Don't denote a source in a psychology paper as "psychologist Anne Smith" or in a literature paper as "literary critic Wayne Booth." But do mention professional qualification, especially where you are quoting, when it isn't apparent from the nature of the course or paper—as Jennie does, in this paper for an ethics course, when she uses a physiologist and a zoologist (lines 9–11). Additionally, do describe the nature of a source that is especially authoritative or distinctive—if it's the seminal article or standard biography, for example, or an especially famous or recent study, or by the leading expert or a firsthand witness.

[F] INDIRECT QUOTING OR CITING: When you haven't actually read the original source, cite the passage as "quoted in" or "cited in" the source in which you found the passage—both to credit that scholar for finding the quoted passage or cited text, and to protect yourself in case he or she has misquoted, quoted out of context, or otherwise misrepresented. Cite a summary account of a text or a topic provided by another source only when that source is a scholarly one (see section 1.2); don't rely on a summary of an academic article or theory, for example, or of a historical phenomenon, that you find on the Web site of an advocacy group. And always read for yourself any source that's crucial to your argument, rather than relying on a summary.

2.3 Rules for Quoting

For both quotations that you embed in your own sentences and quotations that you quote as indented blocks, observe these general rules:

(a) *Quote only what you need or is really striking.* If you quote too much, you may convey the impression that you haven't digested the material or that you are merely padding the length of your paper. Whenever possible, keep your quotations short enough to embed gracefully in one of your own sentences. Don't quote lazily; where you are tempted to reproduce a long passage of several sentences, see if you can quote instead a few of its key phrases and link them with a concise summary.

(b) *Quote verbatim,* carefully double-checking the source after you write or type the words even if you have pasted in the quotation (texts can get jumbled in electronic transmission). Quote verbatim even if the source passage itself is misspelled or ungrammatical, indicating this by adding in brackets after the problematic word or phrase the italicized Latin word [*sic*], meaning "thus": Hemingway wrote that his editor "had a verry [*sic*] nice time at the bar." See Boxes G and H for the few minor exceptions to the rule of verbatim quotation.

(c) *Construct your own sentence so the quotation fits smoothly into it.* Jennie has done this at lines 15–18: *Such a bird has proved, writes Diamond, "that he must be especially good at escaping predators, finding food, resisting disease; the bigger the handicap, the more rigorous the test he has passed."*

(d) *Usually announce a quotation in the words preceding it* (as Jennie does in line 15 with *writes Diamond*) so your readers enter the quoted passage knowing who will be speaking and won't have to reread the passage in light of that information. Announcements before longer quotations should also suggest what the reader should be listening for in the quotation (see 2.4c).

Withholding the identity of a quoted source until a citation at the end of the quotation is acceptable only when the identity of a quoted source is much less important than, or a distraction from, what the source says. This might be the case, for example, if you were giving a quick sampling of opinion—say, in a history paper, giving a series of short quotations illustrating a common belief in the divine right of kings, or in an English paper, quoting from a few representative early reviews of Walt Whitman.

(e) *Choose your announcing verb carefully.* Don't say "Diamond *states*," for example, unless you mean to imply a deliberate pronouncement, to be scrutinized like the wording of a statute or a biblical commandment. Choose rather a more neutral verb ("writes," "says," "observes," "suggests," "remarks," "argues") or a verb that catches exactly the attitude you want to convey ("laments," "protests," "charges," "replies," "admits," "claims," "objects"). Choose verbs carefully when summarizing and paraphrasing sources as well.

(f) *Don't automatically put a comma before a quotation*, as you do in writing dialogue. Do so only if the grammar of your sentence requires it (as Jennie's sentence at line 15 does, whereas her sentence at line 36 does not).

(g) *Put the period or comma ending a sentence or clause after the parenthetical citation*, except after a block quotation (see section 2.4f).

(h) *Indicate clearly when you are quoting a passage* as you found it quoted in another source (see Box F). ,

2.4 Quoting Blocks

If you need to quote more than four lines of prose or two verses of poetry, indent the passage as a block. Jennie does this when she quotes three consecutive sentences of Diamond's book at line 26 (*"I'm strong and I'm superior"*) that give a particularly vivid statement of Diamond's theory. Doing this makes her paper more persuasive by giving her criticisms a specific focus, and it reassures readers that she is not misrepresenting Diamond by selecting a few weak or misleading phrases.

Quote a block only when you will consider closely the language of your source—for example, when discussing a speech by Lincoln, an argument by Kant, an eyewitness account of a revolution, or a key policy statement, but rarely in a science or social science paper—and only when you will follow up your quotation with some commentary on it. Otherwise, long passages of other people's

[G] FITTING QUOTATIONS TO CONTEXT: There are a few cases in which you may need to adjust a quoted passage, in a very minor way, to fit its context in your paper.

(1) **To punctuate the end** of an embedded quotation, use whatever punctuation your sentence requires, not the source author's punctuation. In Jennie's sentence at lines 15–18, Diamond may or may not end his sentence after "passed"; however, since the student ends her own sentence there, she uses a period. *Put a period or comma inside the close-quotation mark*, as in lines 18 and 36 in the excerpt from Jennie; put colons and semicolons outside the close-quotation mark.

(2) **To emphasize** certain words in a quoted passage, in order to make them stand out, place in parentheses after your close-quotation mark the phrase (*my emphasis*) or (*emphasis added*). If the author has italicized the words, indicate this by adding (*Smith's emphasis*).

(3) **To add or change** a word in a quotation to make it fit into the grammar of your own sentence, which you should do only rarely, put brackets [ ] around the altered word. A source passage like "nostalgia for my salad days" might appear in your sentence as *he speaks of "nostalgia for [his] salad days."* A source passage like "I deeply distrust Freud's method of interpretation" might become *Smith writes that he "deeply distrust[s] Freud's method of interpretation."* Use this cumbersome device rarely; always try to construct your sentence so you can quote verbatim. If you need to change only an initial capital letter to a lowercase letter, do so silently, without putting brackets around the letter.

(4) **If the passage you quote contains a quotation,** use single rather than double quotation marks to indicate the source author's quoting.

(5) **To indicate a line break** in a quoted passage of poetry, use a slash (/), inserting a space before and after the slash: *Hamlet wonders if it is "nobler in the mind to suffer / The slings and arrows of outrageous fortune" or physically to act and thus escape them forever.*

voices will drown out your own voice and will take up space that you should be devoting to your own ideas. The basic rules for quoting blocks are as follows:

(a) *Indent all lines 10 spaces (or 1″) from the left margin,* to distinguish a block from a paragraph break. Single-space the block, to distinguish it further from the rest of the text, unless your instructor prefers double-spaced blocks (as do many publications for manuscript submissions).

(b) *Don't put an indented block in quotation marks;* the indenting replaces quotation marks. Only use quotation marks in an indented block where the source author is quoting or is reporting spoken words (as when Homer reports Achilles's funeral oration in the *Iliad*).

(c) *Tell your readers in advance who is about to speak and what to listen for.* Don't send them unguided through a long stretch of someone else's words. Notice how Jennie sets up the block quotation in lines 23–25, telling us beforehand both what we will be listening to and what we should listen for: *Diamond's characterization of the message that human teenagers send by smoking and drinking creates an image of a strutting animal.*

(d) *Construct your lead-in sentence so that it ends with a colon*—pointing the reader ahead (as Jennie does at line 25) to the quotation itself. Occasionally, clarity or momentum may be better served by having your lead-in sentence run directly into your quotation, in which case you may require a comma or no punctuation at all. But this should be the exception, not the rule.

(e) *Follow up a block quotation with commentary that reflects on it and makes clear why you needed to quote it.* Your follow-up—unless you have discussed the quotation in the sentences leading up to it—should usually be a few sentences long, and it should generally involve repeating or echoing the language of the quotation itself, as you draw out its significance. Any quotation, like any fact, is only as good as what you make of it. After her block quotation of Diamond, Jennie follows up at length, echoing the language of the quotation (*"remain alive and healthy,"* line 36) in her analysis of it. Another way to state this rule would be to *avoid ending a paragraph on a block quotation.* End with follow-up commentary that pulls your reader out of the quotation and back into your own argument about the quoted material.

(f) *When using an in-text, parenthetic system of citation, put your citation of a block quotation outside the period at the end of the last sentence quoted.* This makes clear that the citation applies to the whole block, not only to the last sentence quoted. Note that the citation *(199)* comes at the end of the block quotation in line 31 of Jennie's paper.

[H] OMITTING WORDS BY ELLIPSIS: To omit words from the middle of a passage that you are quoting, use ellipsis points: three spaced periods inserted at the point of omission. *"Even to take drugs once or twice,"* Diamond writes, *"I must be strong enough to get past . . . the misery of my first hangover"* (199). If a sentence ends within the omitted portion, add an extra, fourth period and space, before the ellipsis, to indicate this. Don't use ellipsis marks at the start of a quotation, and only use them at the end if you are quoting a block and have omitted words from the end of the last sentence quoted. Don't omit only single words or short phrases, and never omit words in a way that gives a false sense of what the passage says (see section 3.3a). If the text you are quoting itself contains ellipsis marks, put them in square brackets [. . .].

2.5 Using Discursive Notes

Use a discursive or "content" footnote or endnote (a note that includes comments, not just publication information) when you want tell your reader something extra to the strict development of your argument, or incorporate extra information about sources. In the first case, for example, you may want to direct your reader to a further reading or mention the ideas of another writer that are similar to or different from yours:

    5. See chapter 3 of George Folsom's *Rectitudes*
    (London: Chatto, 1949) for an excellent summary of
    Gnostic doctrine and a slightly different critique of
    the ontological argument, stressing agency rather
    than effect.

Or you may want to briefly amplify or explain something you have said, as on p. 11 of this book and in the following example:

> 6. These differences are not small: in 1990 the US spent 45 percent more per capita than Canada, nearly three-quarters more than Germany and three times as much as the United Kingdom (Kingshorn 121; Connors 11).

Or you may want to notice, as an interesting side note, a connection to or implication of your argument that your paper does not develop:

> 12. The use of the word "smelly" in this passage is illuminated by Jeffrey Myers's observation that Orwell "uses odor as a kind of ethical touchstone" (62). Orwell concludes his essay on Gandhi, Myers notes, by remarking "how clean a smell he has managed to leave behind" and says that the autobiography of Dali, the moral antithesis of Gandhi, "is a book that stinks."

Except in a long paper or thesis, however, use such notes sparingly. In most cases, if the note is really interesting enough to include, you should work it into the argument of your paper (or save it for another paper).

Discursive notes that give extra information about sources include notes that announce a nonstandard edition or your own translating:

> 3. All translations from Pasteur are my own; I use the Malouf edition, which is based on an earlier and more complete draft of the treatise.

And notes that explain something about your citing system, your use of terms, or the meaning of your acronyms and abbreviations:

> 5. See chapter 3 of George Folsom's *Rectitudes* (London: Chatto, 1949) for an excellent summary of Gnostic doctrine and a slightly different critique of the ontological argument, stressing agency rather than effect.

> 2. Unless otherwise noted, references to Locke are to *Second Treatise of Government*, ed. C. B. Macpherson (Indianapolis: Hackett, 1980), which is cited by page number only.

3. Dickinson's poems are cited by their number in the Johnson edition, not by page number.

[4]In this paper NK will refer to a natural cell-killer.

And notes that acknowledge an uncited source or influence (see also Box C):

1. My understanding of Reconstruction is influenced by my reading of W. J. Cash's *Mind of the South* (New York: Knopf, 1941) and by discussions with Carol Peters and Tom Wah.

7. I am indebted for this observation and for the term "self-researching" to Susan Lin's comments in Anthro 25 (2/6/98).

1. I wish to thank Roberto Perez for his objections to an earlier draft of this paper, and for directing me to the Gosson article.

1. Work for this assignment was done in collaboration with Vanessa Praz, who is mostly responsible for the "Methods" section.

[6]I owe this example to Norma Knolls, whose help in understanding the mathematics of decision theory I gratefully acknowledge.

[2]In this paper I use an analogy between soul and state developed in Prof. Caroline Hill's lectures for Sociology 144, Howard University, fall term 2003-4.

If you are acknowledging help of a general kind, evident throughout your paper, put the raised reference number for the note immediately after your title or at the point at which you first state your main idea, and put the note at the bottom of your first page or at the beginning of your endnotes. If you are acknowledging help on a specific point, put the note at the bottom of that page, or at the appropriate point in your sequence of footnotes or endnotes.

For all discursive notes, if you are using MLA, APA, or CSE citation style in your paper (see Chapter 4), use superscript numbers for your discursive notes, as in the last two examples above. If you are using MLA style, do not indent the first line of the note; otherwise, do.

3

Misuse of Sources

In addition to other tests you face at college is the moral test of arriving at your own ideas and fully crediting those who help you arrive at them, when it would sometimes be easier to do neither. Passing this test, you grow as a person. Failing it, especially when this involves a deception that violates the trust on which the scholarly community is built, can have serious consequences. This chapter describes some of the ways in which sources are misused and suggests how you can prevent yourself from getting into situations that lead to misuse.

3.1 Plagiarism

In everyday conversation, the fact that some of our thoughts and phrases originate with others is treated casually. The fact is taken more seriously in scholarly conversation, where what may seem like name-dropping to outsiders is actually giving credit. In scholarly writing, when you are making a careful demonstration—the credibility of which depends on a careful distinguishing between what is yours and what is another's—the fact is taken very seriously indeed.

Plagiarism is the act of passing off the information, ideas, or words of another as your own, by failing to acknowledge their source—an act of lying, cheating, and stealing. *Plagiarus* means "kidnapper" in Latin; in antiquity, *plagiarii* were pirates who sometimes stole children. When you plagiarize, as several commentators have observed, you steal the brainchild of another.[1] Because you also claim that it's

---

1. See for example John Ciardi, *Good Words to You* (New York: Harper & Row, 1987), 225; and Lance Morrow, "Kidnapping the Brain Children," *Time,* December 3, 1990, 126.

your own brainchild, however, and use it to get credit for work you haven't really done, you also lie and cheat. You lie to your instructor and other readers of your work, and you cheat both your source of fair recognition for his or her work and your fellow students who have completed the same assignment without plagiarizing.

Plagiarism occurs at every educational institution (Harvard College reports, for example, that in 2006–7 it required 24 students to withdraw for academic dishonesty),[2] but incidents vary in seriousness and in circumstance. Many students have at some point in their careers obliviously or lazily incorporated a few phrases from a source, or simply absorbed a basic idea from a source that should probably have been cited. In such cases, the plagiarized material represents an insignificant contribution to the paper in question. When more substantial sections are involved, occasionally a student has been confused about the rules of acknowledgment. At the other end of the scale is the student who cold-bloodedly plagiarizes entire sections or a whole paper because he or she doesn't care about the course and is unwilling to give it any time.

Most often, however, the plagiarist knows the rules and has started out with good intentions but hasn't left enough time to do the work that the assignment requires. Perhaps the student had even downloaded sources from the Internet earlier, only to find later that the sources answer all of the interesting questions on the topic, or that he or she doesn't understand the material well enough to come up with the kind of paper that the assignment seems to want. The student has become desperate, is too embarrassed to get help or ask for another extension, and just wants the whole thing over with.

At this point, in one common scenario, the student gradually drifts over the moral line into plagiarism, getting careless while taking notes on a source or incorporating notes into a draft. The source's words and ideas blend and blur into those of the student, who at this point has neither the time nor the inclination to resist the blending and blurring. In another common scenario, the student panics and appropriates sections from one or more secondary sources or from another student's work—copying from the source directly and occasionally rephrasing a sentence, or closely paraphrasing the source without providing any citation—hoping to get away with it just this one time.

---

2. *The Administrative Board of Harvard College: A User's Guide 2006–7* (Cambridge, MA: Harvard University, 2006), 43.

From the viewpoint of the university, the gradual line-crossing is no more acceptable than the sudden line-crossing. In both cases, the student is aware that what he or she is doing is wrong and chooses to continue rather than asking for more time or help, or accepting a lower grade for unoriginal but honestly cited work. The consequences of the discovered plagiarism are of course far worse than this (see Box I), and Internet search engines have made discovering plagiarism much easier.

[I] DISCIPLINARY CONSEQUENCES OF MISUSING SOURCES: Not all cases of academic dishonesty are discovered, of course, but many are, and the consequences can be severe. Minor violations are sometimes handled by the course instructor, who may fail the paper or require that the student rewrite it. For more serious cases, the student or students involved will receive a failing grade for the course; in addition, most institutions require instructors to forward suspected cases of plagiarism or other misuses of sources to a disciplinary committee for a hearing. These committees, many of which have student members, are typically thorough and fair. The accused is usually entitled to counsel and advice, has the right to write a statement and appear in person before the committee, and may appeal the decision. The lightest penalties for students found guilty involve a period of probation and a reeducation seminar, in addition to a failing grade in the course. More common is a period of suspension or even permanent dismissal. This can be costly in the short run, in terms of lost tuition, and even more so in the long run: a disciplinary action that involves sources usually results in a permanent mark on the student's record or transcript. Most professional schools, graduate schools, and scholarships also require colleges to report any such infractions in their letters of recommendation, and require students to report them in their applications. This is not to speak of the emotional cost—the process of being discovered or accused is harrowing, and not only a serious distraction from learning for the student but a cause of pain and embarrassment for the family. For specific guidelines and penalties associated with misusing sources, consult your student handbook.

3.2 Forms of Plagiarism

Plagiarism can occur in any kind of paper or presentation, from a short problem set or response paper to a long research paper or thesis. More common than wholesale copying, especially in longer papers, is piecemeal or "mosaic" plagiarism, in which a student mixes words or ideas of a source with his or her own words and ideas, *or* mixes uncited words and ideas from several sources into a pastiche, *or* mixes properly cited uses of a source with improperly or uncited uses. At any point in any paper, however, plagiarism usually takes one of the following forms:

(a) *Uncited data or information:* If you read p. 30 of this book for a paper you are writing on plagiarism in American colleges, and then you say in your paper that Harvard College required 24 students to withdraw for academic dishonesty in 2006–7 and you don't cite this booklet (p. 30), you are plagiarizing information that is not common knowledge. You need to cite such information, again, even when it isn't part of your main argument—when it appears in a "background" section of a paper or in accounts of previous work done on the topic. Your citation must accurately reflect your process: if you claim that you found the information about academic dishonesty at Harvard in the *Administrative Board* volume itself (which you have not read), instead of as cited in *this* volume, you are misleading your reader and possibly embarrassing yourself (see Box F).

(b) *An uncited idea, whether a specific claim or a general concept:* Suppose you read the first paragraph of the previous page and then write this in your paper:

```
Many have attempted to give simple definitions of
plagiarism. Harvey, for example, defines it as
"passing off the information, ideas, or words of
another as your own, by failing to acknowledge their
source."³ But plagiarism is not in fact a simple sin:
rather, it involves the dastardly trio of lying,
cheating, and stealing. Essentially it means
stealing the brainchild — the idea — of another
writer and claiming it as your own, thereby gaining
unfair advantage over others who have done their own
work. "Plagiarism" is a particularly appropriate
word for the theft of brainchildren, since it comes
```

from an ancient Latin word for pirates who stole
young boys and girls.

---

3. *Writing with Sources, Second Edition* (Indianapolis:
Hackett, 2008), 29.

Here you properly cite the quotation in the first sentence, and the Latin etymology of child-stealer given in the last sentence is common (dictionary) knowledge. But the idea of stealing a *brain*child is not common, nor is the claim of the triple sin involved in plagiarism. These distinctive ideas are plagiarized from the final paragraph on p. 29 of this book, even though you present them in a different order and in different words, because they are uncited. Like the "But" that begins your second sentence, your citation in the first sentence of the passage is a deception. It makes readers think that you are fair and scrupulous, and that you have a viewpoint distinct from the source's, when in fact you are being both unscrupulous and unoriginal.

(c) *An unquoted but verbatim phrase or passage:* Suppose that you have read the last paragraph on p. 30 of this book and you write this:

Plagiarism, as Harvey suggests, is often the result
of fatigue and panic. Imagine that it is 3:00 A.M. The
student in question, a good student and certainly not
the kind who would cold-bloodedly plagiarize a whole
paper, has started on his paper too late. By the next
afternoon, he has neither the time nor the
inclination to fight the blending and blurring of his
sources' words into his own. Imperceptibly, he
crosses a moral line.[4]

---

4. *Writing with Sources, Second Edition* (Indianapolis:
Hackett, 2008), 30.

Here you end the passage with a citation that acknowledges a general reliance on the ideas of the source text, thus implying that all of the language is your own. Yet, you have in fact borrowed several distinctive phrases verbatim, without quotation marks: "cold-bloodedly," "neither the time nor the inclination," "blending and blurring," "crosses a moral line." You may fix on certain words in a source as more striking than those around them, but this is all the more reason to give credit for the words by quoting, not simply citing. Beware of this kind of plagiarism, especially when you are summarizing background material that you don't think an "essential" part of the paper, or that you feel the source author has already summarized quite nicely.

(d) *An uncited structure or organizing strategy:* Suppose that, having read p. 30, you write this:

```
The occasions of plagiarism vary. Kim, a foreign
student, simply didn't understand American notions
of intellectual property and citation. In his paper
he relied heavily on the idea of one book, to the
exclusion of his own ideas, thinking that this was
the best way to honor the writer's authority.
Michelle steeped herself so thoroughly in her sources
that, when she wrote her paper, she took over a
fundamental idea in them as a given and accidentally
reproduced some of their most striking turns of
phrase. Eric, having taken invertebrate biology only
because it fit neatly into his schedule, did almost
none of the course reading and simply printed out a
term paper he found on the Internet. Glenn and Sara,
more typical cases, actually liked the invertebrate
course and intended to write good papers for it, but
simply ran out of time to come up with their own
ideas. Hurriedly bringing his paraphrased notes over
into his draft, just a few hours before the deadline,
Glenn started letting his sources' ideas mix in with
his own. About this same time, Sara, who had been
staring at her blank computer screen all morning, was
finally overwhelmed by anxiety and went looking for
the paper her roommate had shown her that she had
written for the same class last year.
```

Your words and details here are indeed original, and the general idea that plagiarism occurs in different circumstances is obvious enough to count as common knowledge and doesn't need citing. You have, however, taken the structural framework or outline of the passage directly from the source passage, which considers patch plagiarizing a result of (a) ignorance of the rules, or (b) oblivious absorption of an idea or replication of a phrase, in addition to (c) wholesale plagiarizing out of indifference or laziness, and (d) plagiarizing in a time panic, either by careless note-taking or deliberate copying. Providing no citation, you plagiarize a distinctive intellectual structure or way of proceeding with a topic—even though, again, your language differs from that of your source and your invented examples are original. You could have fairly introduced this latter fact and been credited for it by saying, for example, "The occasions of plagiarism (as mapped in a general way by Harvey) vary widely."

[J] AVOID AMBIGUOUS CITING: Students who have cited incompletely may find themselves accused of plagiarism. Sometimes an author's name is mentioned in the student paper, at the point at which a source has been drawn upon, but no publication information has been provided in a citation or reference list. Or, author and publication information is provided in a list of references but not cited at the point in the paper where the source is drawn upon. Or, author and publication information are cited for a passage that draws heavily on a specific section of a source, but no page number is provided. These are occasionally real oversights; but when readers are unable to find enough information to allow them to verify a source, they may suspect that the incomplete citing is attempting to disguise an over-reliance on a source—as it sometimes is. Students who then protest that the source *is* mentioned in the paper, and that they were simply sloppy about citing, face the difficult task of proving that their plagiarism was accidental.

3.3 Other Misuses of Sources

(a) *Misrepresenting Evidence:* When you have an idea or interpretation that you wish to be true—especially when the assignment is due shortly—you may be tempted to fudge your evidence to make it seem true. You may be tempted to ignore or sweep under the carpet evidence that you know doesn't fit, in which case you are simply betraying your own intelligence. However, you may also be tempted into more serious violations of academic honesty. You might be temped to quote or paraphrase a source out of context or in misleading excerpts, so it seems to say what you want. You would be doing this if, in your essay on plagiarism in American colleges, you argued that most plagiarism in college papers is accidental, and you wrote the following:

```
Harvey believes that, although sometimes a panicking
paper-writer "has neither the time nor the
inclination" to resist the incursion of a source's
ideas, students are "confused about the rules of
acknowledgment."⁵
```

5. *Writing with Sources, Second Edition* (Indianapolis: Hackett, 2008), 30.

The quoted passages can indeed be found on p. 30 of this volume, but the emphasis there—that only a *few* students are confused—is the opposite of what your summary implies.

Still more seriously, you might be tempted into altering or fabricating a source or some data. Because this kind of deception violates the basic principle of scholarly communities, in which members build on one another's work (the principle of valid reasoning based on true evidence), and because such a deception may suggest an inclination to commit similar acts in later life, it will usually result in serious action by the instructor, the department, or the university.

(b) *Improper Collaboration:* This occurs when two students submit more or less identical written work for an assignment on which they have worked together, and which is not a group presentation. Collaborative discussion and brainstorming is a vital activity for professional scholars; indeed, most articles in the sciences and social sciences have multiple authors. However, the author or authors of articles not only acknowledge in the completed article the contribution of other discussants, they also write the article on their own. When you are asked to collaborate on a project but are required to submit separate papers, you must write up your paper on your own, acknowledging the extent of your collaboration in a note (see section 2.5).

You and your partner, that is, should not compose the report or exam answer as you sit together—instead, you should only take notes. If you divide up aspects of the assignment (assuming the assignment permits this), you should not write up your aspect and e-mail it to your partner, but bring your notes to your meeting. Additionally, you should *discuss* each other's notes, not just photocopy them. Finally, beware of your partner's request, at the last minute and in a panic, to read over your finished report; you may be tempting him or her to plagiarize. Professional scholars do ask one another to read drafts; but again, in these cases only one paper is being produced, not two. If you're unsure about your instructor's policy on collaboration, ask.

(c) *Dual or Overlapping Submission:* Don't take it upon yourself to decide that work you plan to submit for one course, though in many places identical to work you will submit or have submitted for another course, is "different enough" by virtue of small changes you have made (e.g., an added section or an altered introduction or conclusion). When you are running late and need to submit a paper, don't simply submit a cut-and-pasted version of the paper you submitted for another course. Either act will land you in disciplinary trouble. You must first get permission from both instructors for such submissions. Be aware that, should your instructors give you permission for dual submission, they will likely require from you a longer paper than they require of other students in the course.

(d) *Abetting Plagiarism:* You are also guilty of misusing sources if you knowingly help another student plagiarize—whether by letting the student have or copy from your own paper, or by writing a paper or part of a paper for the student (as, for example, when in the course of "editing" a paper for another student, you go beyond correcting mechanical errors and begin rewriting significant portions of the paper). Any of these actions makes you liable to disciplinary action. It is right to be generous and collegial; however, when another student asks you for help with a paper, try whenever possible to phrase your comments as questions that will draw out the student's own ideas.

[K] AVOID ALL-BUT QUOTING: If your own sentences follow the source so closely in idea and sentence structure that the result is really closer to quotation than to paraphrase, you are plagiarizing, even if you have cited the source. You may not simply alter a few words of your source—even of a source such as an abstract you read for a literature review. You need to recast your summary into your own words and sentence structure, or quote directly.

3.4 How to Create High-Risk Situations

Students who misuse sources usually don't plan to. They plan to write thoughtful papers that display their own thinking, but they get themselves into situations in which they either misuse sources from haste or negligence, or they come to believe that they have no choice *but* to misuse sources. Following are some (bad) ideas and attitudes that help create such predicaments.

   1. *"Start late; adrenalin will get you through."* Adrenalin may get you through an all-nighter; but for a substantial paper, starting a week before the due date may be starting late. You will always be surprised by how much thought and work a paper requires. This will be especially true for a paper that you have been putting off because you don't understand the material or simply haven't connected with the course. Procrastinating in such situations is a frequent cause of plagiarism.

   2. *"Don't waste time writing until you know what you want to say."* In most cases, you won't know what you have to say until you do write—until you have jotted and assembled notes (the earlier you begin doing so, however casually, the better) and taken several cracks at formulating your main idea. To prevent a last minute panic, set aside enough time to write a draft and a serious revision. If research is involved, set aside even more time to formulate a question, do research and become temporarily overwhelmed, reformulate your question in light of what your research revealed, then do more focused research. Arriving at an idea is the end of this process, not the start.

   3. *"Just skim the assignment prompt, don't get bogged down in its details."* Such skimming can in fact lead to late realizations and panic. Because even important aspects of an assignment may not be obvious immediately, read the prompt closely and on several occasions. The little time this takes is worth the plenty it can save: a stitch in time saves nine. Read the prompt when you first get it, jotting down initial thoughts or questions and get the topic turning over in your mind; this will allow you to notice relevant material in subsequent reading, lectures, and discussions. When you start taking notes and planning out the paper, read the prompt again to get clear on its goals, especially regarding how much, if any, research is required *or permitted*. Read the prompt yet again when you start

writing, at which point you're in a position to appreciate what the challenges of the assignment really are and what the prompt says about them. (It may provide more definite advice and direction than you first realized, perhaps asking you to focus on a particular aspect of the topic, not to give the breezy overview of aspects you were planning; or to focus on a few primary sources, using secondary sources only for framing or not to use them at all.)

4. "Part of the assignment is guessing what your instructor expects." You do need to find your own way to write the paper; no instructor likes to be asked to "just tell me what you want." It's the instructor's job, however, to make clear the general expectations of an assignment. Instructors, knowing the material and field so well, sometimes think these expectations are obvious when they aren't. If the assignment is confusing on a second read-through, when you've begun to plan and write, contact your instructor and go to his or her office hours. He or she may be able to provide or describe samples of this kind of paper from earlier classes, offer hypothetical theses or approaches, or suggest a good way to get started on the paper. It's up to you to ask for clarification, however. The fact that an assignment doesn't fully explain itself does not excuse plagiarism.

5. "Follow your interest above all." Yes, discovering a topic you care about is one of the keys to good writing. If, however, you decide to write on a topic which, although only tangential to the course or assignment, interests you so much that you're sure the paper will write itself, or about which you have discovered some irresistibly fascinating information, let your instructor know. If you light out on your own away from the assignment, especially if you do so late in the game, you may find yourself unexpectedly at a dead end or in an intellectual swamp. To work your way out, or to work out how your topic in fact does connect to the course, you may need to get an extension. Don't panic and try to solve your problem by plagiarizing.

6. "To get the lay of the land, start every paper by doing an Internet search of key terms and skimming sources that turn up." Although this approach may indeed generate ideas, it's just as likely to overwhelm and paralyze you, alienating you from your own instincts and interests in the topic. Try instead to get down some of your own thoughts and responses early, so you have at least a starting point that is your own and that can help narrow your search. If the assignment itself doesn't ask prompting questions, try free-writing or brainstorming, formulating a hard question for yourself to answer, locating areas of problem or conflict, imagining different viewpoints, or picking a few key passages and annotating them closely.

7. *"Do all your work on-screen, where the action is."* That can be the problem: too much action, not enough thought, since your computer is also where all the distractions are—not just e-mail and the Internet but thousands of further sources to check out. At a certain point, in working online, you should select and print out the main sources you plan to use and sit down elsewhere to read and annotate them. A significant challenge of writing with sources in the Internet age, the age of high volumes and high speeds, is simply to make yourself take time to digest and reflect upon your material with undistracted attention.

For the same reason, print out and take away to read the drafts of papers you write. Hard copy, especially if read aloud, makes it easier to notice problems in your expression and logic. It also makes it harder to ignore a questionable use of sources that may have seemed all right in the freewheeling online world.

8. *"When taking notes on sources, just summarize; come up with your own ideas when you're done.* In fact, this approach may leave you with a lot of summarized ideas and no time left to come up with your own. In general, take notes actively, not passively. Don't just copy down or summarize the source's words or ideas; record your reactions, reflections, questions, and hunches as you go. Note where you find yourself resisting, doubting, or puzzling over what a source says, or connecting it to something else; jot down possible arguments or observations you might want to make. These will provide starting points when you begin to frame the project of your paper, and they will help keep you from feeling overwhelmed by your sources—or your notes. When you do summarize, don't loosely copy source material and simply change a few words; either summarize radically (see section 2.1) or quote exactly, using quotation marks.

9. *"Your paper is your responsibility; hole up and write it."* Yes, writing does tend to be solitary work; but even a little input from others can help greatly. Even if the assignment prompt doesn't require you to write in stages, for a paper of any length you should

[L] INTERNET ETHICS: Working with sources online is no different, morally, than working with sources off shelves. Online sources may give the *impression* of not being anyone's intellectual property. The sheer volume of flowing information and ideas, their apparently merely virtual existence, the ease with which they can be appropriated and manipulated, the project of digitizing the world's libraries into a single pool of knowledge, the constant advances in storage and access technology that make conventions of attribution seem outdated, and attempts to update conventions seem tentative—all these factors contribute to that impression. So does the fact that much of the Internet in fact *is* unregulated, a network of sites freely importing, exporting, and adapting material from one another in spirit of open access, free borrowing, and common ownership. But although human knowledge is indeed the inheritance of all humans, reliable knowledge is gathered, formulated, and established through the efforts of individuals, working in careful and regulated ways. The laissez-faire ethic of the Web may be adequate for amateur assemblages of knowledge; but the scholarly enterprise, whereby painstaking work builds on earlier painstaking work toward truth, requires careful attribution.

try to crystallize your early thoughts into a brief proposal or outline and get a brief response to this from your instructor or classmates (who may want you to return the favor or even to exchange drafts for critique). Getting early feedback from others can help you get unstuck; it can give you ideas or tip you off to problems that, on your own, you may realize too late. And it gives you a living audience to imagine as you write, which can help you imagine what to say.

10. *"During your initial reading of sources, keeping track of publication information will only slow you down, and you may not even use some of the sources."* Here again, time taken early, to save publication data for all sources you read, will repay itself in the late stages of writing when time is short and when—because the book you need may be buried or back on the library shelf—you might be tempted to do the citation from memory or just to skip it altogether. Worse, if you have recorded source ideas anonymously, you may mistake them, willfully or not, for your own. URLs will remain in your browser's history, of course, but that history may get erased. If

you cut and paste a passage from one place to another, you may forget where it came from, or the site may change or disappear; and, more dangerously, the passage may become detached from the source information. For these reasons, you should not only create a bookmark but actually paste the URL to any source material you have copied. Also keep in mind that if questions arise about the source of your ideas, you may be asked to produce your notes, sources, and research process; so keep a hard copy of any key sections of online sources.

11. *"Compose your paper in the file where you collect your sources and notes, so these can be readily drawn in."* In fact, they may be *too* readily drawn in, if you compose this way. The accidental or not-so-accidental blending of source ideas and language into paraphrase, and of paraphrase or summary into argument, is a major cause of plagiarism. When you write with sources, work with three distinct files. Keep source material in one file, with publication information attached. In a second file, keep your notes on sources (your summaries, paraphrases, and commentaries), into which you copy only the most relevant excerpts from the sources themselves—preferably in a different font or color (keep your source language in this font or color throughout the composing process). Compose your paper itself in a third file, bringing in source material as needed for the argument you develop.

12. *"Try to sound impressive and sophisticated, like a real scholar."* Certainly your style will show the influence of the scholars you read and the kinds of moves they make, but don't *try* to sound more learned than you are. Your papers aren't expected to sound just like the articles you read, and indeed your intelligence will emerge most clearly in a plain, direct style. Such a style will also keep clear the distinction between your own thinking and your sources'. Once you begin to appropriate a voice that isn't yours, moreover, it becomes easier to appropriate words and ideas—to plagiarize. It's harder to be dishonest in a plain style than in a fancy one.

You may become paralyzed, especially in a field that's new to you, by an exaggerated idea of what would be an original enough idea for a paper. If this happens, get clarification from your instructor. When working with difficult sources, it can be an achievement simply to summarize plainly and accurately or to integrate your summaries. In such cases, you are usually not expected to resolve

issues that experts have been debating for years, but only to organize the material and clarify the issues, bringing out their complex-
ity, in your own way.

13. *"Don't seek help if you find yourself in a jam; it's humiliating
and will single you out to your instructor as a screw-up."* Plagiarizing, in fact, is a far greater humiliation and singling-out. Whatever
reason has made you feel stuck, confused, or panicked about time—
and there may be many, including problems in your life—let your
instructor know. He or she is spending less time thinking about
your late paper than you imagine, and is more interested in helping
you succeed. The sooner you make contact, the better. Make contact
even if you feel embarrassed that you've let yourself get into the situation again, or because you haven't attended lectures or section, or
think you're the only student in the class who is having trouble (you
aren't). If you feel that you have a special fear or block about writing
papers, or procrastinate excessively, or if you have chronic difficulty
organizing and prioritizing work, make an appointment with a
counselor or psychologist.

14. *"In a pinch, borrow a friend's paper to inspire you, or borrow
some notes to work with."* If you're really in a pinch, reading
another student's finished paper may well discourage or panic
rather than inspire you, and it may tempt you to plagiarize. Instead,
ask the student to help you brainstorm some of your own ideas. As
for borrowed notes, you have no way of knowing their source; they
may come directly from a book or lecture, or from a book discussed
in a lecture.

What you *should* do in a pinch, with all legitimate options
exhausted, is face the music: hand in whatever you have written,
cited honestly, and either ask apologetically for more time to complete the work and accept any grade penalty for this, or just accept
the lower grade you may receive for too much mere summarizing.
That grade will matter far less in the story of your life than will the
consequences of plagiarizing.

[M] ENCOUNTERING "YOUR" IDEA IN A SOURCE: Should this happen, don't pretend that you never encountered the source—but don't panic either. If it's your major idea and you're near the end of work on the paper, finish writing your argument as you have conceived it. Then look closely at the source in question; chances are that its idea isn't exactly the same as yours, that you have a slightly different emphasis or slant, or that you are considering somewhat different topics and evidence. In this case you can either mention and cite the source in the course of your argument (*"my contention, like Ann Harrison's, is that . . ."* or *"I share Ann Harrison's view that . . ."*), but stress the differences in your account—what you have noticed that Harrison hasn't. Go back and reshape your argument slightly, to bring out the different emphasis. If the argument in the source really *is* the same as yours, and you are in the midst of a long paper, go to your instructor, who may be able to suggest a slightly different direction for your paper. If you aren't writing a big paper, and haven't time to recast, use a note of acknowledgment:

> 12. In the final stages of writing this paper, I discovered Ann Harrison's article "Echo and Her Medieval Sisters," *Centennial Review* 26.4 (Fall 1982), 326-40, which comes to the same conclusion. See pp. 331-2.

Don't try to use such a note to cover plagiarism. Your instructor will know from your paper whether you had your own, well-developed idea before reading the source, and may ask you to produce your rough notes or drafts. (To be safe, always hold onto your notes and drafts until a paper has been returned.)

4

Styles of Citation

How you cite sources matters less than when you do, but knowing how makes it easier to cite when you should. This chapter describes several common styles of citation, first giving basic rules of the style and then special cases.

4.1 Documenting a Source

Your basic task in citing is to give your readers enough information to locate and verify any source you use. "Enough" information includes

- the name of the author or authors (or organization, if no author is listed)
- the title of the item (or Web page)
- the name of any volume (or Web site) that includes the item
- the date of that volume's (or site's) publication
- the page number(s) to which you refer (for e-sources, use the paragraph or section number)

When your source is an article in a journal, you also need to give its volume number, issue number (unless the pages run continuously through the volume), and inclusive page numbers of the article. When your source is a book, you need to give the place of publication and (if published after 1900) the name of the publisher. When your source is a Web site, you must give the URL and date of your access or retrieval.

What matters most, however, is that you signal the availability of this information at the point at which you draw on the source, and that you do this in a clear and consistent way throughout your paper. There are a few basic methods of signaling: you can insert a number that refers to a footnote or endnote; you can place in parentheses basic author, year, and page information that refers to a list of references at the end of your paper; or you can insert a code symbol (number or letter) that refers to a list of references.[1]

One or another of these methods is used by the particular citation styles—each favored by a certain group of disciplines or publications—outlined in this chapter and further illustrated in the Appendix. For cases not found here or that cannot be extrapolated from those that are, consult the Web sites of the organizations associated with the styles. The styles are also recognized by Web-based citation programs that can automatically format the publication information you enter (see Box N). To use such programs, however, you need a basic understanding of how at least one signaling style works—and preferably more than one, because different courses may require you to use different styles.

Note that for all of these styles you should start your reference list on a new page after the last page of your text. (Start footnotes, on each page, four lines from the bottom of your last line of text, making sure you stop your text soon enough to fit the entire note on the page). Title your list of entries as follows:

Chicago Manual of Style endnotes	=	*Notes*
MLA author-page citing	=	*Works Cited*
APA author-year citing	=	*References*
CSE author-year citing or coding	=	*References*

If you are required to attach a bibliography to your paper in addition to notes or references, use the MLA or APA format but call the list "Bibliography." Publications prefer that submitted manuscripts be double-spaced within *and* between notes and references, but some instructors prefer that students single-space within notes and references and double-space between them. Inquire about your instructor's preferences.

---

1. A fourth method, used in books written for general audiences, inserts no signals at all in the text. Rather, a "References" or "Sources" section at the end of the book gives cue phrases from earlier passages (e.g., *P. 106 "condemned by many critics"*), each of which is followed by the names of sources, publication information, and sometimes commentary.

[N] CITATION MANAGEMENT PROGRAMS: Software is now available that makes it a matter of a few keystrokes to record and store source information from searches, insert correct citations into a paper, and then create a properly formatted reference list—in whichever one of several hundred journal styles (including those described in sections 4.2–4.5) you choose. These programs create a personal database of materials on the Web and can be accessed from anywhere (unlike resident programs like *Endnote*, which store materials on your computer). They allow you to search databases as you work on your paper, and to store not only references but also notes you've taken on those references, keeping notes and references linked to but separate from sources themselves.

A citation management program is not, however, an automatic citation system. Software can't tell you when to cite, or whether to provide a page number, or even whether or not you should mention an author's name in your sentence—let alone whether that sentence properly distinguishes the author's ideas from your own. This remains your responsibility.

Note also that the advent of these programs means that there is less excuse than ever for losing reference information or allowing it to become detached from your sources, or for not linking reference information to a proper citation in your paper, or for letting your sources blur into your notes.

4.2 Chicago Note Style

In this style, you insert a raised reference numeral into your paper at the end of the sentence in which you draw on a source. This numeral refers your readers to a note at the bottom of the page (footnote) or end of the paper (endnote) that begins with the same numeral and gives information about the source:

```
Diamond suggests that humans share the same
"unconscious instinct" that makes birds give
dangerous displays.[7]
```

Here, the raised 7 refers the reader to the following note—the first line of which is indented—that gives the source and page number:

```
    7. Jared Diamond, The Third Chimpanzee: The
Evolution and Future of the Human Animal (New York:
HarperCollins, 1992), 199.
```

Footnotes (or endnotes) are used in books in all fields, and in papers in the humanities and some social sciences. They add minimal clutter to the body of your paper and disrupt the flow of your sentences less than in-text citation styles.

The arrangement and punctuating of information in the example note above is that stipulated by the University of Chicago Press in its *Manual of Style*. Chicago format for an **online** source is as follows:

```
    27. Conrad J. Bladey, "The Potato Famine in
History," http://www.intl.net/cksmith/famine/
history.html.
```

Chicago style does not put angle brackets around a URL, or require you to give either the date the site was created or the date you accessed it. The Appendix illustrates the Chicago format for many different kinds of sources.

Chicago General Rules

Put your reference number whenever possible at the end of your sentence, outside the period and outside a close-quotation mark that follows the period:

```
Diamond suggests that humans share the same
"unconscious instinct" that makes birds give
dangerous displays.[7]
```

```
Diamond suggests that humans share the same
"unconscious instinct."[1]
```

For clear attribution, however, you may occasionally need to put the reference number within your sentence (where it follows any punctuation except a dash, which it precedes), or to put one number within the sentence and another at the end:

```
Although Jared Diamond suggests that humans share the
same "unconscious instinct" that makes birds give
dangerous displays,[6] others have suggested a more
political explanation for recklessness.[7]
```

To minimize the number of notes in a single passage, you may cite more than one source with a single reference number; however, you should always make clear which source pertains to which part of your sentence, using the "for/see" formula or a similar construction. You might cite Diamond and the "others" together at the end of the sentence in the previous example, and document them in a single note:

```
7. See Diamond's The Third Chimpanzee: The
Evolution and Future of the Human Animal (New York:
HarperCollins, 1992), 192-204. For a more
psychological account, see Melvin Konner, Why the
Reckless Survive — and Other Secrets of Human Nature
(New York: Viking, 1990), esp. 133-37.
```

Citing a source for a second or subsequent time, you need only give the author's surname and a page reference:

```
8. Diamond, 196.
```

If you are using several sources by the same author, use an abbreviated title as well:

```
8. Diamond, Third, 196.
```

Chicago Special Cases

(a) *Referring to a specific passage in a literary work:* Clarity may require you to give the location of the passage in your sentence (*at line 23 he writes . . .*). If not, give this location at the end of your note. For a **poem** of more than 12 lines, give the relevant line number or numbers. For a specific passage in a **novel** or long poem, give the chapter or section number before giving the page number (*Chap. 14, p. 26*). For a passage in a **play in verse,** instead of the page number give the act, scene, and line numbers, separated by periods:

```
6. Hamlet, ed. Harold Jenkins (London: Methuen,
1982), 3.1.56-68.
```

(b) *Reproducing an artwork or illustration:* Refer your readers to the figure or illustration number you have given it (*see figure 4*), and cite the source immediately below the item by artist, title, date, and source data:

```
Illus. 4. Käthe Kollwitz, Home Worker, 1910 (charcoal
16" x 22", Los Angeles County Museum). In Women
Artists 1550-1950, ed. Anne Sutherland Harris and
Linda Nochlin (New York: Knopf, 1981), 264.
```

If you reproduce a table or figure (chart, graph, map, or other illustration) from a source, use the procedure described on p. 77. In a bibliography, if you have one, list artwork by the surname of the artist, and list a chart or graph by the source text's author.

(c) *Submitting a separate bibliography with your paper:* If you are asked to do this, use the formatting for MLA references, illustrated below and in the Appendix.

4.3 MLA In-Text Style

Scholars in some fields prefer that basic source information be available in the text of a paper itself. This information, placed in parentheses and referring to more complete documentation at the end of the paper, includes the author's or authors' last name(s), along with either the specific *page* on which the information, idea, or passage is found (in English and some other humanities fields) or the *year* in which the source was published (in the social sciences and sciences).

The parenthetical style developed by the MLA, a large association of modern literature and language teachers, is an **author-page** style. Because author-page citing keeps the exact page location in the source attached to your use of the source passage in your paper, MLA style works well for papers about longer texts, and for literary or philosophical papers that quote and examine passages closely or include many different passages from the same source.

The author's name may appear in the sentence or in parentheses; the page number always appears in parentheses:

```
Diamond has proposed that self-destructive human
actions are an evolutionary signal of superior powers
(196).

A noted physiologist has proposed that self-
destructive human actions are an evolutionary signal
of superior powers (Diamond 196).
```

These signals in the sentence refer readers to an alphabetical list of "Works Cited," whose entries look like this:

```
Diamond, Jared. The Third Chimpanzee: The Evolution
    and Future of the Human Animal. New York:
    HarperCollins, 1992.
```

The MLA format for **online** sources in your "Works Cited" includes the date the site was produced, or last updated, and, after a period, the date you accessed it and the URL in angle brackets:

```
Saletan, William. "Assembly Required: Constructing
    the First Artificial Life Form." Slate 25 Jan.
    2008. 26 Jan. 2008 <http://www.slate.com/id/
    2182573>.
```

The date of composing or last revising is always followed by the date of access, although the latter is not named as such. MLA formatting for many different kinds of sources is provided in the Appendix.

MLA Basic Rules

Whenever a source's particular formulation of ideas is important to your argument, give the author's name in your sentence:

```
Jared Diamond proposes that self-destructive human
actions are an evolutionary signal of superior powers
(196).
```

```
As Diamond says, "the bigger the handicap, the more
rigorous the test he has passed" (196).
```

Doing this also has the advantage of minimizing clutter at the end of your sentence. Note that the parenthetic citation goes *inside* the period that ends your sentence (except when quoting a block; see section 2.4f) and that, after a quotation, the citation goes outside the close-quotation mark, since it isn't part of the quotation. When you aren't discussing or quoting a source, you may put the name inside the parentheses with the page number:

```
Public concern about smoking appeared much later
(Schmidt 29).
```

When it's necessary to make clear that one part of your sentence comes from a source but another part from you (or another source), you may insert your reference mid-sentence. Put it at a natural pausing point, and inside the punctuation that ends the clause:

```
Although public concern about smoking appeared much
later (Schmidt 29), it appeared precisely when the
advertising campaigns did.
```

MLA style assumes that a number following a name is a page number and not part of a name; do not put *p.* for "page" or *pp.* for "pages" or insert a comma between the name and the page number. If the idea or information you cite comes from two or more sources, however, use a semicolon to separate them in your citation *(Brill 103; Costa and Lerner 132)*.

MLA Special Cases

(a) *Source in several volumes:* Give the volume number and a colon before the page reference, as in *(2: 347)* or *(Winslow 2: 347)*.

(b) *Using more than one work by the same source:* Put an abbreviated title of the source in your citation, to indicate which of the texts you refer to—here, *The Third Chimpanzee:*

```
Jared Diamond proposes that self-destructive human
actions are an evolutionary signal of superior powers
(Third 196).
```

(c) *Source with multiple authors:* For two or three authors, mention all of the names in the signal phrase in your sentence or put them in your parenthetic citation: *(Baker, Smythe, and Wills 207)*. For more than three authors, use the first surname with *et al.* ("and others") in your sentence or in your citation: *(Belenky et al.)*.

(d) *Source listing no author:* Use an abbreviated form of the title. An anonymous article called "Lost Tribes of the Gobi" might be cited as *("Lost" 88)*.

(e) *Quoting a source you found quoted by another scholar,* a source you know only from that quotation: Cite the source as "qtd. in" that scholar:

```
During the walk, according to Keats, Coleridge
"talked without stopping" (qtd. in Murray 66).
```

(f) *Referring to a particular passage in a poem, novel, or play:* For a novel or poem, give the chapter or line number after the page number, following a semicolon:

```
In "Mending Wall," Frost at first does not seem
ironic when he says that "good fences make good
neighbors" (52; 1.27).
```

For a play in verse, cite the act, scene, and line numbers (separated by periods) instead of a page number:

```
When Hamlet says "O heart, lose not thy nature," he
means by "nature" his filial feeling (3.3.351).
```

After block quotations, however, put the parenthetical citation outside the final period.

(g) *Reproducing an artwork or illustration:* Direct your readers to the figure or illustration number that you have given it *(see figure 5)*. Beneath the item, give the artist's full name, then the name of the work and its date. If your paper focuses on the artistic medium, include the medium of the work, its dimensions, and its location or owner:

```
John F. Kensett, Sunset with Cows, 1856. Oil on
canvas, 36 x 39 inches.
```

In your list of works cited, document the source from which you have taken the item, according to #29 in the Appendix. If you reproduce a chart, table, graph, or map, use the format illustrated on p. 77.

4.4 APA and CSE In-Text Styles

Although citation styles in the social sciences and sciences tend to vary from publication to publication, most follow **author-year** style. In a psychology or biology paper, the year of publication matters more than the page number, because you are usually citing articles for their main idea or finding—not for a particular aspect or section, or for the wording of a particular passage (although a page number should be added for quoted or extensively paraphrased material). Moreover, you are often citing authors who have written many short papers on a subject, in a steady process of developing, testing, and correcting hypotheses, and your readers want to know as they are reading whether you refer to later or earlier work.

In your paper, author-year style looks like this:

```
Recent explanations suggest that such actions are
evolutionary signals of superior powers (Diamond,
1992).
```

This is the author-year style for the social sciences that was developed by the American Psychological Association (APA). The author-year style recommended by the Council of Scientific Editors (CSE) is similar but in general slightly plainer. It does not insert a comma in the citation, for example, between author and year:

> Recent explanations suggest that such actions are evolutionary signals of superior powers (Diamond 1992).

In both APA and CSE styles, the information in parentheses refers to an alphabetical list of "References," in which the date of publication is placed prominently, immediately after the author's name, which is emphasized by the indentation of all lines in a citation after the first. Following are examples of **APA** references:

> Diamond, J. (1992). *The third chimpanzee: The evolution and future of the human animal*. New York: HarperCollins.

> Gottesman, C. (1999). Neurophysiological support of consciousness during waking and sleeping. *Progress in Neurobiology*, 59, 469-508.

Note that these styles capitalize only the first significant word of a book or article's title and any proper nouns; they do not place titles of articles in quotation marks. CSE is here again plainer, however. Whereas APA italicizes the titles of journals, magazines, and books, CSE does not; neither does it place a comma between the author's last name and initial or place parentheses around the date of publication. Here are some examples of **CSE** references:

> Diamond J. 1992. The third chimpanzee: The evolution and future of the human animal. New York: HarperCollins. 325 p.

> Gottesman C. 1999. Neurophysiological support of consciousness during waking and sleeping. Progress in Neurobiology 59:469-508.

For a book, CSE style requires you to include at the end of your reference the total number of pages (or inclusive page numbers if you refer only to a section of the book).

For **online** sources, APA and CSE formats again have minor differences, but here APA is simpler:

```
Saletan, W. (2008, January 25). Assembly required:
   constructing the first artificial life form.
   Slate. Retrieved January 26, 2008, from http://
   www.slate.com/id/2182573
```

The publication date given in APA is that of initial creation or copyright *or* the most recent update; date "retrieved" is given in month-day-year order. There is no period after the URL. CSE includes a few more features:

```
Saletan W. 2008. Assembly required: constructing the
   first artificial life form. Slate [magazine
   online]. [revised 2008 Jan 25; cited 2008 Jan 26].
   Available from: http://www.slate.com/id/2182573
```

CSE format inserts *Available from:* before the URL and places the date of access before the URL, in year-month-day order. It includes a revised date in square brackets in addition to the creation date, and a description of the source medium after the date (e.g., [serial online], [journal online], [monograph online], [Internet]). Further samples of APA and CSE formats may be found in the Appendix.

[O] CITING FREQUENTLY USED SOURCES: When you write a paper that closely analyzes, or refers repeatedly to, one or a few texts, you can use a note to signal **an abbreviated form of citation.** You can do this in the following ways:

```
    1. Unless otherwise noted, references to Locke
are to The Second Treatise of Government, ed. C.
B. Macpherson (Indianapolis: Hackett, 1980),
which will be cited by page, chapter, and section
number.

    2. Act, scene, and line numbers refer to
Hamlet, ed. Harold Jenkins, Arden edition
(London: Methuen, 1982).

    3. Page references to NA refer to Stevens's The
Necessary Angel: Essays on Reality and the
Imagination (New York: Knopf, 1951); CP is his
Collected Poems (New York: Knopf, 1955), and OP
his Opus Posthumous, ed. Samuel French Morse (New
York: Knopf, 1957).
```

Such a note allows you to cite the source each time (by page, section, or line number, or abbreviation plus page, section, or line number) without having to footnote or supply author and date each time. Having provided the third note above, you might write later in your paper, *In one early poem, he sees the imagination is as a "bottle of indigo glass" (OP 22).*

When you refer to the **same source repeatedly in a paragraph** or passage, you need not repeat the citation at the end of every sentence but only when you refer to a different page in the source or start a new paragraph of your paper (as Jennie, on p. 19, doesn't give a page reference for lines 15–18). Note, however, that your language needs to constantly make clear where you are drawing on a source—not giving your own ideas—by using phrasing like *"Aristotle further observes that. . . ."* It isn't enough, when your paragraph draws repeatedly on a source, simply to give a single citation at the start or end of that paragraph—unless you cast each sentence so as to preclude any ambiguity as to where the words, ideas, or information come from.

APA/CSE Basic Rules

When you mention the author's name in your sentence, insert the year of publication immediately afterward, or at the end of the sentence, or at the end of the relevant clause—whichever makes clearer which are the source's thoughts and which are yours:

```
Schmidt (1984) notes that public concern appeared
much later.
```

```
Schmidt notes that public concern appeared much later
(1984), yet it appeared precisely when the major
advertising campaigns did.
```

The parenthetical citation always comes inside the punctuation that ends your own sentence or clause.

In science and social science writing, the idea or information cited at a given point often comes from two or more sources. Put the sources in alphabetical order, separated by a semicolon: in APA *(Schmidt, 1984; Tritt & Spank, 1985)* or in CSE *(Schmidt 1984; Tritt and Spank 1985).* If the two sources are by the same author, arrange them in chronological order, separated by a comma: in APA (*Schmidt, 1984, 1990*) or in CSE (*Schmidt 1984, 1990*).

It is also common, in science and social science writing, to cite repeatedly sources with **multiple authors:**

- If **two authors,** cite both authors' names each time you cite: APA (*Balough & Stearns, 1988*) or CSE (*Balough and Stearns 1988*).
- If **three to five authors,** cite the first time using all of the authors' surnames: in APA (*Belenky, Clinchy, Goldberger, & Tarule, 1986*) or CSE (*Belenky, Clinchy, Goldberger, and Tarule 1986*). In subsequent citations, cite only the first surname followed by *et al.* in APA (*Belenky et al., 1986*) and by *and others* in CSE (*Belenky and others 1986*).
- If **six or more authors,** cite by the first author's surname and *et al.* or *and others* from the start.

In both APA and CSE, if you quote or refer to a specific passage, or paraphrase a particular section of a book at length, include the page number(s) in your parenthetical citation. In APA, insert a *p.* for "page" or *pp.* for "pages":

```
As Diamond (1992) observes, "the bigger the handicap,
the more rigorous the test he has passed" (p. 196).

Schmidt notes that public concern appeared much later
(1984, pp. 23-24).
```

APA/CSE Special Cases

(a) *Author is an organization with a long name:* Name it the first time in full, followed immediately by brackets containing the abbreviation that you will use in parentheses in all subsequent citations: (U. S. Department of Health and Human Services, 1989) [USDHHS].

(b) *No author listed:* Use a one- or two-word abbreviation of the title in your citation: (*Lost Tribes, 1990*). For CSE style, omit the comma.

(c) *More than one source by the same author and year:* Cite and document the first source as (*Stearns & Wyn, 1990a*) and the second source as (*Stearns & Wyn, 1990b*). For CSE style, omit the comma.

(d) ***Reproducing an illustration, chart, or table:*** In APA style, identify the item by placing above it a figure or table number, a title, and any required explanation. Put your citation below the item, starting with the word "Source" or "From," if you copy directly; "Redrawn from" if you redraw; and "Modified from" or "Adapted from" if you have made even minor changes. Then give the name, publication data, and page number, including the source again in your reference list:

Figure 4. Performance by three groups of children on nine memory tasks. N = children of normal academic achievement; LD-N = learning-disabled children who performed in the average range on short-term memory tests; LD-S = learning-disabled children who performed poorly.

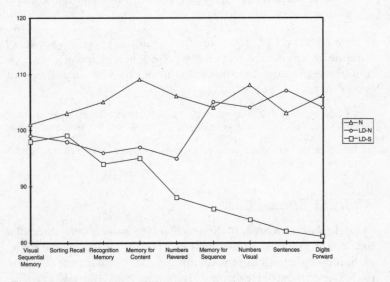

Source: Farnham-Diggory, S. (1992). *The learning-disabled child*. Cambridge, MA: Harvard University Press, p. 121.

(e) ***Personal communication:*** Unless it can be retrieved or accessed by others, don't include in your reference list a personal interview you conducted, a letter or e-mail message you received, or a conversation you had. Give the information only in your text as follows in APA style:

```
A lawyer for the teachers, Diana Scholtz, said that
the action had been pending for several years
(personal communication, April 1, 2007).
```

4.5 CSE Coding Style

Some journals in the sciences require authors to identify each of their sources by a symbol or marker—usually a number but sometimes an initial letter of one or more author surnames. This number or letter appears in (parentheses) or [brackets] or as a superscript[E] in the paper each time that source is referred to, and it refers to a list of "References" at the end of the paper. Often, sources are coded by order of their first mention in the paper (by citation sequence). This sentence cites the third source mentioned in the paper:

```
Recent explanations have suggested that such actions
are evolutionary signals of superior powers (3).
```

Even if this source is cited again, later in the paper, it is still identified by its code number (3), and it appears third in your list of references. In another version of the method, sources are coded by their number in an alphabetic list of references—in which case, the *(3)* in the example above would refer to the third source in the alphabetic list, rather than a citation-order list. Or, if you were coding by initials, Diamond might be cited at the end of the sentence as [D], and listed beside the symbol [D] in an alphabetical list of references. An article by Wallace, Dobbs, and Hershey might be coded as [WDH].

Like footnoting, coding has the advantage of requiring little apparatus in your text; like parenthetical citing, it eliminates the need to make a separate note each time you use a certain source—but it eliminates parenthetical information as well. Coding is appropriate for papers in the sciences, including biology, physics, chemistry, and math, where sources are mostly brief articles from which you don't directly quote, and in cases where you are not citing a great many sources (for which the coding system would become unwieldy).

If you aren't required to use the coding style of a particular publication, use the CSE version described here. To place citations in your paper, assign each source a number based on the order of first mention in your paper, and place the reference numbers in parentheses (or, if you prefer, use raised numerals—as you would for footnotes). If possible, place the numbers at the end of your sentences, but place them elsewhere if necessary for clarity. When you refer to several sources in the same citation, arrange them in descending order of relevance or importance to your point:

> In accordance with published protocols (12, 3, 8–10),
> purification of VP2 was performed identically.

When you refer to a source with three or more authors, abbreviate it in your sentence as the first surname plus *et al.*:

> As Garcia et al. have shown, the new interpretation
> fails to account for a key variable (3).

If you cite a personal communication (in a conversation, letter, or e-mail message), give the information in your paper, not in your list of references:

> Recent attempts by the same laboratory to duplicate
> this result have been unsuccessful (W. Deeb, personal
> communication, 6 April 2003).

If you use a table or figure (graph, chart, or illustration) from a source, use the CSE procedure described on p. 77.

For your reference list, use the format for CSEc shown in the Appendix. Note that this format differs from that of CSE in-text style. It places the first line of each entry, starting with the coding number, flush with the left margin and begins subsequent lines in the entry under the first letter of the name.

> 3. Diamond J. 1992. The third chimpanzee: The
>   evolution and future of the human animal. New
>   York: HarperCollins. 325 p.
>
> 4. Gottesman C. 1999. Neurophysiological support of
>   consciousness during waking and sleeping. Progress
>   in Neurobiology 59:469–508.

Appendix

Listing Your References

Oral, Visual, and Multimedia Sources

[P] COMMON VARIANT SITUATIONS IN LISTING

- *Two authors?* Begin as follows:

  CMS   Carla Williams and Robert O. Castle,

  MLA   Williams, Carla, and Robert O. Castle.

  APA   Williams, C., & Castle, R. O.

  CSE   Williams C, Castle RO.

- *Three authors?*

  CMS   Henri S. Witt, Albert B. Lingren, and
         Willard Dobbs,

  MLA   Witt, Henri S., Albert Lingren, and Willard
         Dobbs.

  APA   Witt, H. S., Lingren, B. H., & Dobbs, W.

  CSE   Witt HS, Lingren BH, Dobbs W.

- *Four or more authors?*

  CMS   Kim-Sung Moon et al. [or use "and
         others"]

  MLA   Moon, Kim-Sung, et al.

  APA   Moon, K.-S., Kirk, C., Sana, P., Regal, L.,
         & Lin, D.

  CSE   Moon K-S, Kirk C, Sana P, Regal L, Lin D.

- *Repeated author?* List entries by the same author, in APA and CSE styles, in chronological order, and repeat the author's name or names in second and subsequent entries.

In CMS and MLA, list entries alphabetically by title, and use three dashes instead of author name:

> Geertz, Clifford. *The Interpretation of Cultures*. New York: Basic Books, 1973.
>
> ———. *Works and Lives: The Anthropologist as Author*. Stanford: Stanford UP, 1988.

- *Group or corporate author?* Use the group, organization, or corporation name instead of author name, e.g., American Historical Association, Minzano Inc., American Institute of Physics. If you abbreviate the group name in your paper, in CSE style, begin the reference with the acronym in brackets, followed, for in-text style but not CSEc, by the full name:

> [AIP] American Institute of Physics. 1990. Style manual. 4th ed. New York: American Institute of Physics. 136 p.

In a CSE coded (CSEc) list, use the abbreviation only.

- *No author, editor, or organization given?* Start the citation with the title of the source. List the item according to the title's first word (not counting *a, an,* or *the*), following the style's general practice for handling titles.

- *Indirect Source?* For a source you cite parenthetically as "qtd. in" (MLA) or "as cited in" (APA) another scholar, list publication data for the other scholar. In CMS, give data for the original source *and* for the other scholar, linked by the phrase "quoted in" or "cited in":

> 1. Claude Levi-Strauss, *The Raw and the Cooked: An Introduction to a Science of Mythology* (New York: Harper & Row, 1969), 18, quoted in Howard Gardner, *Frames of Mind: The Theory of Multiple Intelligences* (New York: Basic Books, 1983), 103.

- *Online source?* Break a long URL immediately before a dot or after a backslash, never mid-word or mid-phrase. If a URL is very long (more than a full line), try to shorten it by making clear the last one or two file sections of the address in the text of your paper instead.

Articles and Short Texts

1. *Article in a journal*

CMS   1. Ann Harrison, "Echo and her Medieval Sis-
ters," *Centennial Review* 26, no. 4 (Fall 1982):
326-40.

MLA   White, Hayden. "Foucault Decoded: Notes from the
Underground." *History and Theory* 11 (1973):
23-54.

APA   Kahneman, D., & Tversky, A. (1979). Prospect theory: An analysis of decision under risk.
Econometrica, 47, 263-291.

CSE   Farber E, Rubin H. 1991. Cellular adaptation in
the origin and development of cancer. Cancer
Res 51: 275-276.

CSEc   1. Farber E, Rubin H. Cellular adaptation in the
origin and development of cancer. Cancer Res
1991; 51: 275-276.

Journals paginated by issue, not cumulatively over the volume:
Include issue number after the volume. Do this in CMS by inserting
a comma and "no." before the issue number (see example above),
and in APA and CSE by putting the month after the year, followed
by the issue number in parentheses. Note also that APA style italicizes volume number, as part of the title, but it does *not* abbreviate
journal titles, as CSE does (see Box Q).

Electronic form of a print journal: In APA, add *[Electronic version]*
after the title of the article.

Library database: In APA, add to the article information the date of
access and the name of the database: *Retrieved April 20, 2007, from
Expanded Academic ASAP database.* In MLA, add the names of the
database, vendor, and library; the date of access; and the URL
enclosed in angle brackets: *Academic Search Premier. EBSCO. Lamont
Library, Harvard College. 21 Apr. 2007* <http://epnet.com/>.

CD-ROM database: In MLA, add to the article information the
name of the database, the medium, the publisher, and the date of
disc: *Proquest General Periodicals.* CD-ROM. UMI-ProQuest. June
2000.

Citing only an abstract of the article: (a) When it's from the original source, insert *[Abstract]* after the title of the article; (b) when it's from a collection of abstracts, add to the end of the citation the name and volume of the collection of abstracts and the volume and page or the item number: *Abstract obtained from Psychological Abstracts, 67, Item 1121;* (c) when it's from a database, insert *Abstract from* after the citation, and follow the database formats already given. For an abstract of an unpublished talk, give the date of delivery before the reference number in the database.

[Q] ABBREVIATING PUBLICATION DATA: Don't include words like *Publishers, Co.,* and *Inc.* in your reference. In MLA style, abbreviate *University Press* to *UP* and journal titles that are commonly referred to by an acronym (*ELH, CCC*). Abbreviate words in journal titles only in CSE style, and only when the title contains two or more words. Follow the guidelines for abbreviation supplied by the National Information Standards Organization (http://www.niso.org).

2. Article in a magazine or newspaper

CMS 5. John Garamendi, "Clinton Offers a Managed Health-Care Plan," *New York Times,* October 8, 1992, late edition, A20.

MLA Walinksky, Adam. "The Crisis of Public Order." *Atlantic Monthly* July 1995: 39-54.

APA Shales, T. (1988, July 20). The Jackson triumph. *The Washington Post,* pp. C1, C6.

CSE Margolis M. 1988 August 12. Thousands of Amazon acres burning. New York Times. B1, B8.

CSEc 5. Margolis M. Thousands of Amazon acres burning. New York Times, 12 August 1988: B1, B8.

Don't include a volume number for newspapers or magazines. Note that APA puts "pp." before page numbers of a newspaper article or anthology item, but not of a magazine or journal article.

Online version of a printed paper or magazine: Add *[Electronic version]* after the title.

Editorial or letter to the editor: In CMS, add "editorial" or "letter to
the editor" after the author's name. In MLA, add "Editorial" or
"Letter to the Editor" after the title of the piece. In APA, add *[Editorial]* or *[Letter to the editor]* after the title but inside the period.

3. Article in an online journal, magazine, or newspaper

CMS   7. Jack Shafer, "Don't Call It Plagiarism:
        Obama's Sound Bite, Considered." *Slate*, February
        25, 2008, http://www.slate.com/id/2184070.

MLA   Shafer, Jack. "Don't Call It Plagiarism: Obama's
        Sound Bite, Considered." *Slate* 25 Feb. 2008.
        19 Feb. 2008 <http://www.slate.com/id/
        2184070>.

APA   Shafer, J. (2008, February 19). Don't call it pla-
        giarism: Obama's sound bite, considered.
        Slate. Retrieved February 19, 2008, from
        http://www.slate.com/id/2184070

CSE   Shafer J. 2008. Don't call it plagiarism: Obama's
        sound bite, considered. Slate [magazine
        online]. [revised 2008 Feb 25; cited 2008
        Feb 27]. Available from: http://www.slate.com/
        id/2184070

CSEc   3. Shafer J. Don't call it plagiarism: Obama's
        sound bite, considered. Slate [magazine
        online]. [revised 2008 Feb 25; cited 2008 Feb
        27]. Available from: http://www.slate.com/id/
        2184070

These examples are for a magazine. For identifying the issue of a
periodical or newspaper, use the formats illustrated in #1.

4. Article, chapter, or item in a collection or proceedings

CMS   3. Richard Rodriguez, "The Achievement of
        Desire," in *The Essay: Old and New*, ed. Edward
        P. J. Corbett and Sheryl L. Finkle (Englewood
        Cliffs, NJ: Blair-Prentice Hall, 1993), 173.

MLA   Goldsmith, Oliver. "The Deserted Village." *The
        Norton Anthology of English Literature*. 5th
        ed. Ed. M. H. Abrams et al. New York: Norton,
        1986. 2507-17.

APA   Salmond, A. (1974). Rituals of encounter among
           the Maori: Sociolinguistic study of a scene.
           In R. Bauman & J. Sherzer (Eds.), *Explorations*
           of the ethnography of speaking (pp. 192-212).
           Cambridge: Cambridge University Press.

CSE   Hanawalt PC. 1987. On the role of DNA damage and
           repair processes in aging: evidence for and
           against. In: Warner HR, editor. Modern biolog-
           ical theories of aging. New York: Raven Press.
           p. 183-198.

CSEc   3. Hanawalt PC. On the role of DNA damage and
           repair processes in aging: evidence for and
           against. In: HR Warner, editor. Modern biolog-
           ical theories of Aging. 183-198. New York:
           Raven Press; 1987.

List by item author, not the editor of the collection—unless you're citing the whole volume, in which case cite by the name of the editor or editors, abbreviating "editor" or "editors" as shown.

Item from published conference proceedings: Follow the provided formats, but give inclusive page numbers of the item before place of publication and publisher.

Item excerpted in a class sourcebook: If you haven't consulted the original place of publication, use as volume title: *Sourcebook for Science B-35, Wetland Ecology, Prof. Jill Hurt. Colby College (Waterville, Maine), Fall Semester 2007.* Give inclusive page numbers for the original publication and in the sourcebook.

5. Item or chapter in a collection of the author's work (no separate editor)

CMS   4. D. H. Lawrence, "Tickets, Please," in *Col-*
          lected Stories (London: Heinemann, 1974), 314-25.

MLA   Hazlitt, William. "On Religious Hypocrisy." In
          The Round Table. London: Dent, 1964. 131-38.

APA   Geertz, C. (1883). "Art as a cultural system."
          Local knowledge: Further essays in interpre-
          tive anthropology (pp. 94-120). New York:
          Basic-Harper.

CSE   Gould SJ. 1977. Ever since Darwin: reflections on
        natural history. New York: Norton. History of
        the vertebrate brain; p. 186–191.

CSEc   4. Gould SJ. Ever since Darwin: reflections on
        natural history. New York: Norton; 1977. His-
        tory of the vertebrate brain, p. 186–191.

6. Preface, introduction, or foreword

CMS   8. Havelock Ellis, preface to *The Sexual Life
        of Savages,* by Bronislaw Malinowski (New York:
        Harcourt Brace, 1929), xi.

MLA   Ellis, Havelock. Preface. *The Sexual Life of Sav-
        ages.* By Bronislaw Malinowski. New York: Har-
        court Brace, 1929. vii–xiii.

7. Review

CMS   7. Robert A. Huttenback, review of *Race and
        Empire in British Politics,* by Paul Rich, *Ameri-
        can Historical Review* 93 (April 1988): 154.

MLA   Leys, Simon. "Balzac's Genius and Other Para-
        doxes." Rev. of *Balzac: A Life,* by Graham Robb.
        The New Republic 20 December 1994. 26–27.

APA   Geiger, J. (1987, November 8). [Review of the book
        And the band played on]. *The New York Times
        Book Review,* 9.

8. Article in an encyclopedia or other reference work

CMS   6. John Fleming, Hugh Honour, and Nikolaus
        Pevsner, eds., *The Penguin Dictionary of Archi-
        tecture,* 2nd ed. (Harmondsworth: Penguin, 1972),
        s.v. "fillet."

CMS   6. *Encyclopaedia Britannica,* 11th ed., s.v.
        "Magna Carta."

"S.v." means *sub verbo,* "under the word."

MLA   "Hannibal." *The Columbia Encyclopedia.* 6th ed.
        New York: Columbia UP, 2001.

APA   Lichen. (2001). In *The Columbia encyclopedia* (6th
        ed.). New York: Columbia University Press.

Article credited to a specific author: In MLA, add that name to the start of your citation: "Ott, William."

Online work (e.g., Encyclopaedia Britannica Online*):* Add retrieval information as shown in #3.

Subscription service: Add the date of access and keyword.

9. Legal case

CMS   6. *Hill v. Cox*, 135 U.S. 11, 21 (1967).

MLA   Watson v. Dunhill Inc. 135 USPQ 88. 2nd Cir 1967.

List cases by title; also give the volume number and abbreviated name of the reporting service, starting page number in the volume, cited page number(s), court that decided the case, and year. Consult *The Bluebook: A Uniform System of Citation,* cited under "Law" in "Further Information" at the end of this appendix.

10. Interview

CMS   3. Candace Caldwell, "Lust of the Eye," interview by Malcolm Strong, *Visual Arts,* June 1995, 23–29.

MLA   Caldwell, Candace. Interview with Malcolm Strong. "Lust of the Eye." *Visual Arts* June 1995: 23–29.

APA   Strong, M. (1995, June). "Lust of the Eye." [Interview with Candace Caldwell]. *Visual Arts,* 23–29.

11. Letter in a published collection

CMS   9. Virginia Woolf to Emma Vaughan, 12 August 1899. *Congenial Spirits: Selected Letters of Virginia Woolf,* ed. Joan Trautman Banks (San Diego: Harcourt Brace, 1989), 5–6.

MLA   Montagu, Lady Mary Wortley. "To Alexander Pope." 7 September 1718. *Selected Letters.* Ed. Robert Halsband. New York: Viking-Penguin, 1986.

12. *Letter or papers from an archive*

CMS   10. Ralph Young to David Simms, 11 May 1922,
            Ralph Waldo Young Papers, Harvard University
            Archives, Pusey Library, Cambridge, MA.

MLA   Campbell, David. Papers. Perkins Library, Duke
            University, Durham, NC.

Put the title of an archived item that *has* a title (such as a memorandum) in quotation marks. For an interview transcript, add the interviewer and date.

13. *Personal letter*

CMS   20. David Gewertz, letter to the author, September 8, 2006.

MLA   Gewertz, David. Letter to the author. 8 September 2006.

In APA and CSE, don't list a personal letter as a reference; instead, cite it in your paper as *(D. Gewertz, personal communication, September 8, 2006)* for APA, or as *(8 September 2006)* for CSE. In all styles, cite such a letter as a source only if you are acknowledging a debt or if you can provide a copy of the text, should a reader request it.

14. *E-mail*

CMS   20. Edgar Bowers, e-mail to the author, September 5, 1995.

MLA   King, Marla. E-mail to the author. 16 April 2007.

In APA and CSE, don't include an e-mail message in your reference list; instead, cite it in your paper as *(M. King, personal communication, April 16, 2007)* for APA, or as *(16 April 2007)* for CSE. In all styles, cite such messages as sources only if you are acknowledging a debt or if you can provide a copy of the text, should a reader request it.

15. *Section or page of a Web site*

CMS   27. John Fraser, "Cold White Peaks and Sung
            Foothills," *Nihilism, Modernism, and Value* sec.
            II, http://www.jottings.ca/john/peaks.html.

MLA   Fraser, John. "Cold White Peaks and Sung Foot-
       hills." *Nihilism, Modernism, and Value.* Sec.
       II. June 2001. 21 January 2008. <http://
       www.jottings.ca/john/peaks.html>.

APA   Brin, D. (1993, May 2). The good and the bad: Out-
       lines of tomorrow. Retrieved September 5,
       2000, from http://www.kspace.com/KM/spot.sys/
       Brin/pages/piece1.html

CSE   Brin D. 1993 May 2. The good and the bad: outlines
       of tomorrow [Internet]. [cited 2000 Sept 5].
       Available from: http://www.kspace.com/KM/
       spot.sys/Brin/pages/piece1.html

CSEc   6. Brin D. The good and the bad: outlines of
       tomorrow [Internet]. 1993 May 2 [cited 2000
       Sept 5]. Available from: http://
       www.kspace.com/KM/spot.sys/Brin/pages/
       piece1.html

Web log (Blog) entry: In APA, insert the name of the Web log after
the item title. In MLA, insert *Web log posting* after the item, followed
by a period, the sponsoring organization (if any), the name of the
Web log, and a period.

16. Posting to an archived discussion group

CMS   Ralph Jacobs, post to Africa in the News
       Forum, May 14, 2005, http://www.africanewsonline.
       com/forums/forumsdisplay.php?f=14.

MLA   RadioMan. "Re: Against Guns." Online posting. 3
       May 2005. Weapons List. 4 September 2006.
       <weaponslist—og@email.regent.edu>.

APA   Smith, K. (1995, April 12). Statement of
       principles [Msg 23153]. Message posted to
       libdis@wtu.edu

Only messages that are archived should be included in the APA references list.

Books and Reports

17. Book

CMS   1. Judith N. Shklar, *Ordinary Vices* (Cambridge, MA: Belknap-Harvard University Press, 1984), 39.

MLA   Trimpi, Wesley. *Ben Jonson's Poems: A Study of the Plain Style*. Stanford: Stanford UP, 1962.

APA   Gardner, H. (1983). *Frames of mind: The theory of multiple intelligences*. New York: Basic Books.

CSE   Woese CR. 1967. The genetic code: the molecular basis for genetic expression. New York: Harper & Row. 486 p.

CSEc   1. Woese CR. The genetic code: The molecular basis for genetic expression. New York: Harper & Row; 1967. 486 p.

Edition other than the first: If the title page indicates that you are using an edition other than the first, indicate the designated edition immediately after the title: *2nd ed.* in CMS or MLA, or *(2nd ed.)* in APA.

Published before 1900: Omit the name of the publisher (some publications in history and classics omit it for all books).

Published by a smaller branch or imprint of a large company (e.g., Belknap, of Harvard University Press; Anchor, of Doubleday): Cite both, as in CMS example in #17.

Information missing (publisher, place, or date): Indicate this with the abbreviations "n.p." (no publisher, no place) or "n.d." (no date).

18. Book with author(s) and editor(s)

CMS   12. W. H. Auden, *Selected Poems*, ed. Edward Mendelson (New York: Vintage, 1979), 79.

MLA   Forster, E. M. *Commonplace Book*. Ed. Philip Gardner. Stanford: Stanford UP, 1985.

APA   Freud, S. (1971). *The psychopathology of everyday life* (J. Strachey, Ed.). New York: Norton.

19. Book in several volumes

CMS   13. Sandra Gilbert and Susan Gubar, *No Man's Land,* 2 vols. (New Haven: Yale University Press, 1988), 1:90.

MLA   Orwell, George. *Collected Essays, Journalism, and Letters*. Ed. Sonia Orwell and Ian Angus. 4 vols. London: Secker and Warburg, 1970.

APA   Field, J. (Ed.). (1960). *Handbook of physiology* (Vol. 3). Washington, DC: American Physiological Society.

20. Reprinted book

CMS   14. Booker T. Washington, *Up From Slavery: An Autobiography* (1901; repr., New York: Doubleday Page, 1978), 34.

MLA   Wilder, Thornton. *The Bridge of San Luis Rey*. 1927. New York: Washington Square, 1969.

APA   Allport, G. W. (1979). *The nature of prejudice*. Cambridge, MA: Addison-Wesley. (Original work published 1954)

21. Online book

CMS   12. Lewis Carroll, *Alice's Adventures in Wonderland* (New York: Millenium, 1991), http://quake.think.com/pub/etext/1991/alice-in-wonderland.txt.

MLA   Carroll, Lewis. *Alice's Adventures in Wonderland*. New York: Millenium, 1991. 21 Jan. 2007 <http://quake.think.com/pub/etext/1991/alice-in-wonderland.txt>.

APA   Johnson, E. (1997, June 3). *No exits. Platforms of the future*. Retrieved September 20, 2006, from http://carol.cdma.books.com/6666/pof.htm

22. Book in a series

CMS   15. Carl Jung, "Anima and Animus," in *Aspects of the Feminine,* trans. R. F. C. Hull, Bollingen Series 20, Vol. 27 (Princeton: Princeton University Press), 85-100.

MLA   Peterson, Margaret. *Wallace Stevens and the Ide-*
           alist Tradition. Studies in Modern Literature
           24. Ann Arbor: UMI Research Press, 1983.

APA   Tannen, D. (1989). Talking voices: Repetition,
           dialogue, and imagery in conversational dis-
           course. In J. J. Gumpertz (Ed.), *Studies in*
           interactional sociolinguistics 6. Cambridge:
           Cambridge University Press.

If a **series editor** is listed, supply that name after the series name, as
in the APA example.

23. *Translated book*

CMS   16. Friedrich Nietzsche, *The Gay Science,*
           trans. Walter Kaufmann (New York: Vintage, 1974),
           86.

MLA   Rousseau, Jean Jacques. "The Origin of Civil
           Society." *The Origin of Civil Society: Essays*
           by Locke, Hume, and Rousseau. Trans. Gerald
           Hopkins. Ed. Sir Ernest Baker. New York:
           Oxford UP, 1947. 212-68.

APA   Durkheim, E. (1957). *Suicide* (J. A. Spaulding & G.
           Simpson, Trans.). Glencoe, IL: Free Press.

24. *Dissertation*

CMS   11. Yael Leah Maschler, "The Games Bilinguals
           Play: A Discourse Analysis of Hebrew-English
           Bilingual Conversation" (PhD diss., University of
           Michigan, 1988), 23-25.

MLA   Joyce, Joseph Patrick. "An Econometric Investiga-
           tion of Government Preference Functions: The
           Case of Canada 1970-1980." Diss. Boston U,
           1984.

APA   Goffman, E. (1953). *Communication and conduct in*
           an island community. Unpublished doctoral dis-
           sertation, University of Chicago.

CSE   Rush WF. 1972. The surface brightness of
           reflected nebulae [dissertation]. Toledo (OH):
           University of Toledo.

CSEc   2. Rush WF. The surface brightness of reflected
        nebulae. Ph.D. dissertation, University of
        Toledo, 1972.

Published dissertation: Treat as a book (see #17), but include before
the publication data the designation *diss.*, the university, and the
year. Note that APA italicizes even an *un*published dissertation.

Citing only an abstract of the dissertation: First, give full information for the dissertation; then, after a period, give the name and volume of the collection of abstracts, the date, and the item number:
Dissertation Abstracts International, 54 (1993): 1360B.

25. Government publication

CMS   17. U.S. Bureau of the Census, *Historical Sta-*
        tistics of the United States: Colonial Times to
        1870 (Washington, DC: GPO, 1975), 185.

MLA   U.S. Bureau of the Census. *Historical Statistics*
        of the United States: Colonial Times to 1870.
        Washington: GPO, 1975.

APA   U.S. Department of Health and Human Services.
        (1990). *Healthy people: The surgeon general's*
        report on health promotion and disease preven-
        tion (PHS Publication No. 79-55071). Washing-
        ton, DC: Author.

26. Congressional record

CMS   *Congressional Record,* 100th Cong., 1st sess.
        1987, Vol. 70, pt. 2:687-95.

MLA   *Cong. Rec.* 8 Feb 2000. 1222-46.

APA   S. res. 103, 107th Cong., Cong Rec. 5844 (2001)
        (enacted).

27. Technical or research report

APA   Williams, S., & Tibble, D. (2001). Teaching with
        technology (ASCHE ERIC Higher Education
        Report, 3). Washington, DC: George Washington
        University.

CSE   Williams S, Tibble D, editors. 2001. Teaching
       with technology. Washington, (DC): George
       Washington University. ASCHE ERIC Higher Edu-
       cation Report, 3.

CSEc   5. Williams S, Tibble D, editors. Teaching with
       technology. (ASCHE ERIC Higher Education
       Report, 3). Washington, DC: George Washington
       University, 2001.

Oral, Visual, and Multimedia Sources

28. *Lecture, conference paper, speech, or performance*

CMS   19. Helen Vaughan, "Robert Lowell" (lecture,
       Stanford University, Stanford, CA, November 12,
       2003).

MLA   *Othello*. By William Shakespeare. Dir. Jill
       Davies. Perf. Newtown Players. Lyttle
       Theatre, Somerville, MA. 3 June 1993.

APA   Waters, M. (1993, April 20). *Local labor
       lore*. Paper presented at the annual meeting
       of the Columbus Ethnographic Society, Colum-
       bus, OH.

CSE   Whitaker H. 1982 July 12. Automaticity. Paper
       presented at the Conference on Formulaicity.
       Linguistic Institute, University of Maryland.

CSEc   7. Whitaker H. Automaticity. Paper presented at
       the Conference on Formulaicity. Linguistic
       Institute, University of Maryland. 12 July
       1982.

Performances may also be listed by their playwright, composer, or
individual artist, followed by an abbreviation that indicates role
(e.g., *cond., dir., chor.*).

29. *Artwork, illustration, map, chart, or table*

List a particular map, table, graph, chart, or plate by the title given
in the text, followed (in MLA, APA, and CSE) by a word indicating

the nature of the item and, if published in a book, its page and figure or plate number (if any):

CMS   7. Wendy Otten, "Holland Canal," *Waterways*
(New York: Sparshot, 1985), 12, fig 2.

MLA   *Bear Habitat Before Columbus*. Map. Jennifer Tye.
The Way It Was. San Francisco: Rollins, 1990.
34.

APA   *Visual orientations* [Chart]. (1990). Madison:
University of Wisconsin, Office for Health and
Wellness. Figure 12.

CSE   Office for Health and Wellness. 1990. Visual orientations [chart]. Madison: University of Wisconsin. Figure 12.

If the item is credited to an individual other than the book's author, list by that individual's name. For artwork, give the museum, gallery, or owner; then (unless you're referring to the work as viewed on site) add publication information. In MLA:

Kollwitz, Käthe. *Home Worker*. Los Angeles County
Museum, Los Angeles. *Women Artists 1550-1950*. Ed.
Anne Sutherland Harris and Linda Nochlin. New
York: Knopf, 1981. Plate 107.

30. Film

CMS   24. *Rashomon*, DVD, directed by Akira Kurosawa
(1959; New York: Daiei, 1999).

MLA   *In the Trenches*. Dir. Lionel Askins. Narr. Albert
Hamel. Videocassette. Cityfilm, 1992.

APA   Kurosawa, A. (Director). (1959). *Rashomon* [Motion
picture]. Tokyo: Daiei.

APA   Askins, L. (Director). (1992). *In the trenches*
[Videocassette]. New York: Cityfilm.

DVD or videocassette: Insert a description of medium, as shown in the film examples.

Paper on the work of a director or performer: List by the name of that individual work (as in the APA example).

31. Musical recording

CMS   23. Wolfgang Amadeus Mozart, *The Magic Flute*,
Vienna Philharmonic, cond. George Solti, Decca
compact disc 3988.

MLA   Mozart, Wolfgang Amadeus. *The Magic Flute*. Cond.
George Solti. Decca CD 3988, 1970.

APA   Shocked, M. (1992). Over the waterfall. On *Arkan-
sas traveler* [CD]. New York: PolyGram.

Paper on conducting or performance: List the piece by conductor or performer. In MLA, Solti, George, cond. *The Magic Flute*. Wolfgang Amadeus Mozart. . . .

A particular song or segment of a recording: Give the item name before the recording title (see APA example above).

Musical score or sheet music: Replace performance and production information with the score's place of publication, publisher, and year.

Liner notes: List by the author of the notes, followed by the title of the notes, then the name of the recording and other information.

32. Television or radio program

List **television programs** by producer or by title; give the network in place of the publisher or production company. For an individual episode of a continuing program, try to give the date of the first airing. If citing a televised **interview,** cite by the person interviewed (for CMS and MLA styles) or by the person interviewing (for APA), as in #10.

33. Personal or telephone interview

CMS   20. Edgar Bowers, personal interview with the
author, September 5, 1990.

MLA   Rice, Betina. Telephone interview. 6 March 1993.

In APA and CSE, don't list an unpublished personal interview as a reference; instead, cite it in your paper as *(B. Rice, personal communication, March 6, 1993)* for APA, or as *(6 March 1993)* for CSE. In all styles, cite such a source only if you are acknowledging a debt or if you can provide a copy of the text, should a reader request it.

34. Audio, video, or graphic files from the Internet

MLA   Garcia, Rodrigo, dir. "All Happy Families." 2004. *The Sopranos*. 4 Apr. 2006 <http://www.hbo.com/sopranos/episode/season5/episode56.shtml>.

APA   Aretha Franklin: A life of soul. (2004, January 23). *NPR Online*. Retrieved April 30, 2004, from http://www.npr.org/templates/story/story.php?storyId=1472614

35. Poster session

APA   Richards, D. (2004, May). *Hiring habits of recently hired female supervisors*. Poster session presented at the annual meeting of the American Sociological Association, Washington, DC.

36. CD-ROM

MLA   Hagen, Edward, and Philip Walker. *Human Evolution: A Multimedia Guide to the Fossil Record*. CD-ROM. 2002 ed. New York: Norton, 2002.

MLA   *The Norton Anthology of English Literature Audio Companion*. CD-ROM. 2 discs. New York: Norton, 2001.

Further Information

Many of the following works are available online; simply conduct a search to ascertain the most recent edition. For additional, journal-specific formatting styles, citation management programs can also be consulted.

General and Humanities

Gibaldi, Joseph, and Walter S. Achert, eds. *MLA Handbook for Writers of Research Papers*. 6th ed. New York: Modern Language Association, 2003.

Holoman, D. Kern. *Writing about Music: A Style Sheet from the Editors of 19th-Century Music*. Berkeley: University of California Press, 1988.

Turabian, Kate L. *A Manual for Writers of Term Papers, Theses, and Dissertations*. 7th ed. Chicago: University of Chicago Press, 2007.

University of Chicago Press. *The Chicago Manual of Style*. 15th ed. Chicago: University of Chicago Press, 2003.

Social Sciences

American Anthropological Association. "Style Guide and Information for Authors," *American Anthropologist* (1997): 774–79.

American Political Science Association. *Style Manual for Political Science*. Rev. ed. Washington, DC: APSA, 2001.

American Psychological Association. *Publication Manual of the American Psychological Association*. 5th ed. Washington, DC: APA, 2001.

American Sociological Association. "Editorial Guidelines." On the inside cover of the *American Sociological Review*.

Linguistics Society of America. "LSA Style Sheet." Appears every December in the *LSA Bulletin*.

National Education Association. *NEA Style Manual for Writers and Editors*. Rev. ed. Washington, DC: NEA, 1974.

Natural and Applied Sciences

American Institute of Physics. *Style Manual Instructions to Authors and Volume Editors for the Preparation of AIP Book Manuscripts*. 5th ed. New York: AIP, 1995.

American Mathematical Society. *Author Resource Center.* <http://ams.org/authors>.

Bates, Robert L., Rex Buchanan, and Maria Adkins-Heljeson, eds. *Geowriting: A Guide to Writing, Editing, and Printing in Earth Science.* 5th ed. Alexandria, VA: American Geological Institute, 1995.

Council of Science Editors. *Scientific Style and Format: The CSE Manual for Authors, Editors, and Publishers.* 7th ed. Reston, VA: CSE, 2006.

Dodd, Janet S., ed. *The ACS Style Guide: A Manual for Authors and Editors.* 2nd ed. Washington, DC: American Chemical Society, 1997.

Institute of Electrical and Electronics Engineers. *IEEE Standards Style Manual.* Rev. ed. New York: IEEE, 2005.

Medicine

Iverson, Cheryl, et al. *American Medical Association Manual of Style.* 9th ed. Baltimore, MD: Williams, 1998.

Patrias, Karen. *National Library of Medicine Recommended Formats for Bibliographical Citation.* Bethesda, MD: U.S. Department of Health and Human Services, 1991. For electronic formats see www.nlm.nih.gov/pubs/formats/internet.pdf.

Law

Harvard Law Review, et al. *The Bluebook: A Uniform System of Citation.* 18th ed. Cambridge, MA: Harvard Law Review Association, 2005.

Government Documents

Garner, Diane L. *The Complete Guide to Citing Government Information Resources: A Manual for Social Science and Business Research.* 3rd ed. Bethesda, MD: Congressional Information Service, 2002.

Business

American Management Association. *The AMA Style Guide for Business Writing.* New York: AMACOM, 1996.